Performance Management

— in the —

21st Century

Solutions for Business, Education, and Family

Performance Management

— in the —

21st Century

Solutions for Business, Education, and Family

Dr. Norman Jones

S^{t}_{L}

St. Lucie Press

Boca Raton   London   New York   Washington, D.C.

Library of Congress Cataloging-in-Publication Data

Jones, Norman, 1936–
    Performance management in the 21st century : solutions for
business, education, and family / Norman Jones.
            p. cm.
        Includes index.
        ISBN 1-57444-244-9 (alk. paper)
        1. Industrial efficiency. 2. Mental efficiency. 3. Performance.
    I. Title.
    HD56.J66 1999
    658—dc21
                                                                98-32268
                                                                    CIP

© 1999 by CRC Press LLC
St. Lucie Press is an imprint of CRC Press LLC

No claim to original U.S. Government works
International Standard Book Number 1-57444-244-9
Library of Congress Card Number   98-32268
Printed in the United States of America   1 2 3 4 5 6 7 8 9 0
Printed on acid-free paper

"What is clearly going to be needed in the 21st century, particularly with the diversity in the work force, is the ability to inspire . . . Inspirational leadership is going to become very critical."

Kenneth Chenault

21st Century Leadership

Foreword

Humans have a wide range of potential functioning—from low to high performance. Could there be a more important question for a leader-manager to have answered than, "What can I do to encourage people to function at their highest levels?" Haven't you found yourself functioning differently in different environments? An individual's varying performances can't be explained by his or her genes or his or her past environment, since in both your low and high performance milieu, you were the same genetic you with the same past experiences.

What explains our job satisfaction and our performance?

There is no way out but to accept Dr. Norman Jones' thesis that the leader, manager, or teacher plays a major role in creating conditions to increase performance. The wise author uncovers *the spirit killers* and observes their persuasiveness in our culture. Jones writes, "Spirit killing is so much a part of our culture that few people can recognize the exact event or just how the spirit of a person begins to tail off into an 'I don't care' attitude." Perhaps you can recall some spirit killing events in your own work life, moments when your reason for being at work regressed from filling your self-actualization needs to just making money to pay bills.

No doubt you have been frustrated when attempting to motivate someone and tried praising them to death, yet it didn't work. Why? Dr. Jones articulates the little known but powerful difference between extrinsic and intrinsic motivation. The overuse of praise can be a spirit killer because it builds dependency on the praiser. A person's performance drops when the praiser, the external source of motivation, isn't present. Encouragement, as opposed to praise, builds long-term intrinsic motivation. That is, the person is motivated by internal pushes and pulls, not external praise, punishment, and fear. Talk about building responsibility in people!

I found Jones' comments on how we mistakenly reverse cause and effect to be particularly insightful and, for me, motivating. Throughout the book he shows us examples of where we attribute cause when, in fact, we are experiencing effects. Consider his quote of Jim Tunney, a former NFL official, who said, "Winners don't have a good attitude because they win (effect); they win because they have a good attitude (cause)!" Think about it.

Jones' ideas are steeped in the practical and positive concepts of Alfred Adler and Abraham Maslow en route to developing the science of human relationships. Throughout the book, Jones gives clear strategies to live up to his opening quote of FDR's: "Today we are faced with the pre-eminent fact that if our civilization is to survive, we must cultivate the science of human relationships . . . the ability of people of all kinds to live together and work together in the same world, at peace."

In your own way, in your own personal, family, workplace, community, and global setting, you can acquire Jones' democratic attitude to become more effective with anyone whom you want to help to function at that higher level—as opposed to the lower level—of his or her possibilities.

And then you will be the change that you want to see in the world. Thank you, Norman!

Dr. Lewis E. Losoncy
Author, *The Motivating Team Leader*

Preface

I
t is a fact that research regarding the psychology of management, leadership, motivation, encouragement, and human development has been sadly neglected for nearly 70 years in the major institutions in the United States.

The content of this book explains how and why the rigid, top-down approach to managing and motivating people was once effective, but now causes widespread demotivation, apathy, and insecurity. Those in charge of managing businesses, schools, and, yes, families, must begin to realize that they often create discouraging, nervous, and insecure environments in which people attempt to develop their talents. This tension causes the lack of productivity that corporate boards and CEOs, school administrators and parents, proclaim they want to overcome.

Exactly how this tension is created and what can be done about it is the focus of this book. It shows how workplaces, schools, and families can be transformed to create harmonious environments more conducive to high levels of productivity. Research regarding leadership, motivation, management, and so on is traced from 1927 and reveals that its neglect has been costly to America.

As the global economy increases competition for the United States, it will be necessary sometime in the twenty-first century for the United States to rethink the way it goes about developing its people. Research into how people are best motivated will then be given more priority.

Chapter 1, "The Unseen Enemy," describes how misconceptions about leadership, management, and human development have become an enemy to society, but are difficult to detect. Chapter 2, "The Spirit Killers," shows how the atmosphere in our institutions can be improved through a change in language—a change in the way people talk to each other—that can raise the spirits of people. This was alluded to years ago in the book *In Search of Excellence* when research by Peters and Waterman noted that, "In the good companies the language was different." They maintained that in our institutions, "A true people orientation can't exist unless there is a special language to go with it."

In Chapters 3, 4 and 5, a compelling case is made as to how many of our major institutions, namely businesses, schools, and families, are in jeopardy. They are in trouble because the rigid management within them fails to pay attention to research in leadership, management, motivation, human development, and organizational psychology. Leaders in these institutions have become unapproachable.

Millions of people seek an escape from the tense environments in our institutions and turn to drugs and alcohol which, in turn, can lead to violence, apathy, gang activity, homelessness, abused children, declining motivation in our schools, fragmented families, and other ills. Needless lawsuits arise from such tension. America has become its own worst enemy because of the way it develops its people. This book shows how changes can be made to create harmonious institutions that research infers are a must if America is to remain competitive in a global economy in the twenty-first century.

The Author

Dr. Norman Jones is now retired. He graduated from high school in Marion, IN in 1954, where he was awarded the Kiwanis Achievement Award for basketball. He earned a B.A. degree in Education from Ball State University and a M.A. in Counseling and Guidance, then pursued a career in coaching, teaching, and counseling. He earned varsity letters in basketball at Ball State and went on to become a head coach in high school in basketball, baseball, and golf.

In 1977, he earned a doctorate in Counseling and Educational Psychology from the University of Mississippi. In 1981, he published his first book, *Keep in Touch*, with Prentice-Hall. He founded Communications Unlimited, Inc. and began making presentations on motivation, communication, human development, leadership, management, teaching, and parenting for organizations around the Chicago area. He appeared on WBBM-TV (CBS) in Chicago on the talk show *Common Ground*, and was on WIND and WBBM radio talk shows.

Dr. Jones assisted with adult career education workshops while at the University of Mississippi. He taught graduate courses, including human development for secondary school administrators at Roosevelt University in Chicago and principles of guidance at Northeastern Illinois University. He is the past president of the Northwest Suburban Chapter of the Illinois Guidance and Personnel Association and is a charter member of the Northern Illinois Association for Educational Research, Evaluation, and Development.

He has made presentations for numerous schools, companies, and organizations such as Allstate, Blue Cross and Blue Shield, the Illinois State Board of Education, the International Graphoanalysis Society, and the University of Wisconsin football staff.

Dedication

This book is dedicated to my family, first and foremost to my loving wife, Pat, for her encouragement and her work on the book. It is also dedicated to my three lovely daughters and their husbands and children. They are Mrs. Denise Luksetich and her husband, Rick, and sons, Eric and Adam; Mrs. Diane Stratton and her husband, Eric, and son, Jack; and Mrs. Deborah Struck and her husband, Bob.

The book is also dedicated to those people who were inspirational to me during my years of employment as well as to those who were less than inspirational. All contributed to my ideas about management, motivation, leadership, human development, education, and parenting.

Acknowledgments

Sometimes special people come into our lives and help us meet a goal, overcome a difficulty of some kind, or just encourage us to go forward. Earl Roberts, sales director of the TaleWins Literary Agency, is such a person. Without his assistance in revising my book and making a proposal for its sale, the book might still be in manuscript form. Earl and his TaleWins business administrator, Charlotte Harris, helped make my dream come true. I am forever grateful.

Len Ziehm, neighbor, friend, and sportswriter for the *Chicago Sun-Times*, provided expert editing as the book developed. His work on the book and his encouraging words about its contents made me keep working hard to get it published.

Bill "Barney" Schultz, golf partner, longtime friend, and former colleague, with his great command of the English language, helped answer many questions about writing. This is the second book Bill has helped me publish, and I am indebted to him.

Golfing friends Wayne Nelson, Bill Cannon, and Dick Semelsberger all worked for large corporations, and their input was more than significant. Jim Weakly made a very important contribution. The help of these friends is greatly appreciated.

Marc and Mayme Jo Denny, friends for over thirty years, introduced me to the computer world years ago. They not only taught me how to use the word processor, but also loaned me their computer to start the book. Marc taught me that "unions are caused; they don't just happen," and his words helped motivate me to write this book.

R. A. Keenan provided valuable writing expertise when I had difficulty early on getting my ideas into writing. Her expertise moved the book from idea form to manuscript form.

Pat Bethel, the media department chair at Hoffman Estates High School IL, helped me find material that made the book meaningful. Her assistance is appreciated.

I would be remiss if I did not thank my doctoral instructors at the University of Mississippi who taught me a great deal of what is contained in the book. A heartfelt thanks goes out to my advisor and friend, Dr. Dudley Sykes, Dr. F. J. Eicke, Dr. Grady Harlan, and Dr. Philip Cooker.

A special thanks goes to Dr. Lewis Losoncy, who wrote the foreword and has written many books on management, motivation, leadership, human development, and encouragement. His writings and those of his colleague Dr. Don Dinkmeyer have been an inspiration to me.

A special note of thanks goes out to Bob and Debbie Struck for their computer expertise and the many hours they spent with me after their workdays were over.

Finally, Drew Gierman, the business editor at St. Lucie Press, is the person every author hopes to find while attempting to publish his or her work. An author will always need an editor who first reads the manuscript and then likes it enough to fight hard to get it published. Drew did that for me, and I am very grateful for his effort.

Hardworking people at St. Lucie Press (CRC Press LLC) who were very helpful to me in the publication of this book are: Susan Zeitz, (Project Editor), Carolyn Spence, Anthony Martin, Gerry Jaffe, Carolyn Lea, Pat Roberson, and Elena Meyers.

Contents

1 The Unseen Enemy

Introduction

In 1945, President Franklin D. Roosevelt warned the nation,

> *Today we are faced with the pre-eminent fact that if our civilization is to survive, we must cultivate the science of human relationships . . . the ability of people of all kinds to live together and work together in the same world, at peace.*

During World War II, the United States rose to a challenge with a dedication seldom seen in the history of the world. We defeated an overwhelming enemy. It is now evident and unfortunate that President Roosevelt's warning has been forgotten. We have not risen to the challenge of cultivating human relationships that President Roosevelt deemed important to us.

Since Americans have neglected the warning, we are now faced with an explosion of violence, child and spousal abuse, health care and pension problems, runaway divorce rates, and alcohol and drug abuse. Gangs often rule our streets. Homeless people as well as problems of the elderly and the handicapped are constant news topics. Downsizing, unemployment, and age, sex, and racial discrimination in the workplace are a plague to American citizens. Corruption in government is common. People are not living and working together as President Roosevelt envisioned they should.

In the 1980s the federal government published a report about education titled *A Nation at Risk*. It strongly suggested that education in America was lagging well behind that of other countries. A follow-up report in the 1990s did not show much improvement. Instead of cultivating human relationships, modern day business attempts to motivate employees by using the threat of expendability to gain optimum productivity.

In the past, when faced with such problems to overcome, Americans have proven their desire and ability to solve them. Jonas Salk's effort to conquer the dreaded disease polio was a monumental humanitarian accomplishment. Americans were first to the North and South Poles, first to have telephone conversations, and first to read by electric lights. America has seen its people develop to the extent that some were the first to fly at Kitty Hawk, across the ocean, and to the moon; we even sent an explorer to Mars. Scientists at Oak Ridge developed the atomic bomb that turned back an enemy that threatened our entire population. Why then are we losing the battle to so many problems in our society?

Edward R. Murrow may have said it best:

The obscure we see eventually, the completely apparent takes longer.

These ills in American society are the results of an insidious enemy that has so far defied identification. If we are to confront this villain, it must be made less obscure to all. In the following pages this invisible enemy will be deliberately exposed and defined, and its dangers will be explained.

Confusing Cause and Effect

One tool our enemy uses is the constant practice of making sure we confuse causes and effects in our minds. Various spin doctors in the country have been able to deflect identification of the unseen enemy by blaming different facets of our society for our problems. Television is a prime example. Once considered a scientific marvel, television is now often projected as public enemy number one. Congress often acts as one spin doctor by blaming television as a major cause of violence, all kinds of crime, and illicit sex in the United States. It has urged the television and movie industries to clean up their acts or be sanctioned by the government.

Most agree that violence and sex viewed on television does leave a lasting impression on young people. People over fifty can recall that Elvis Presley's hip movements could not be shown to the viewing public during his performance on the *Ed Sullivan Show*. Compared to the movies now available on cable television, Elvis's gyrations were closer to the motions of the Tennessee waltz.

The increased explicitness is harmful, but modern television is an effect and not the cause of the formidable force strangling the most valuable resource of our nation—its people.

Science and technology are often blamed for the nation's social, economic, and psychological problems. Some will argue that science and math experts have, like a hurricane, swept people into a sea of high tech, causing complicated problems. Automation has cost many Americans their jobs; the Chicago area is running out of area codes; and people have been stalked and even killed as a result of contacts on the internet. Robots have begun replacing people in the workplace, and automation produces everything from automobiles to colas, from beer to clothes and digital watches. High powered x-ray equipment can penetrate through bodies. Strange guns, looking like weapons from Buck Rogers comic strips of years ago, now help supermarket clerks read prices and calculate grocery bills.

Blaming high technology is a popular way to explain away what the enemy is accomplishing instead of properly identifying it. High-tech research does eliminate jobs, and proponents argue that the consequences of people being unemployed creates feelings of tension and anxiety. It is easy to be convinced that by creating full employment for everyone, we could eliminate our problems. It is unfortunate that our invisible enemy is more destructive than the monster of unemployment.

School systems rival television and technology for first-place honors in receiving the blame for America's social problems. Teachers and administrators shift the blame to parents, saying there is no support from the home. Those who blame public schools can point to federal, state, and local governments that control funding. Cause must be more readily identified instead of just giving more money to school districts if we are to win this war with our unseen enemy.

Many people blame peer pressure for our problems in the school system. They believe peer pressure is so severe and teaching methods so inefficient that (as President Reagan suggested in the 1980s) young people must be subjected to old-fashioned discipline if they are going to achieve in school at a level comparable to their mothers and fathers.

Some people say the legal system, from the local traffic court to the United States Supreme Court, has turned the country into an oppressive state. They proclaim that the system invades privacy, caters to the rich, and often benefits criminals by passing laws that limit individual and group freedoms. These issues promote distrust in the legal system; citizens then develop the attitude that they cannot fight city hall and that their government will not help them. They begin to view themselves in a submissive role, approaching their employment as a necessary evil to make money and function within the system.

Others insist the responsibility for the plight of the United States lies at the door of the business and technical schools because of their mediocre training. Some point the finger at the government for exercising inappropriate control and interference with red tape, mandates, and regulations to the extent that the spirit of the people is so drained that they cannot function as the high achieving, independent, and assertive people they are.

The Collective Cop-Out

All of these perceived causes have negative effects on America's society; but they are, collectively, a cop-out so people can avoid confrontations with the real forces causing America's vast social problems.

These cop-outs are not usually deliberate attempts by people to escape the obvious. They are excuses, subconsciously originated, to avoid introspection and the subsequent discovery of how the number-one resource in America—its people—is wasted. America's people are the force that made America great. Do we not have the responsibility to keep it great? An unwillingness to participate in that responsibility means we are ready to accept a decline in living standards.

It is imperative that we unleash the type of energy that people showed in World War II in order to face this challenge of eradicating mediocrity. We must do so with the intent of reinstating the United States to the number one position in the world in business, education, and family structure. Time is growing short. If we are to survive as a nation, we must accomplish this early in the twenty-first century or be swept aside.

Where Do We Turn for Help?

The most important aspect of America's survival will be getting a better effort out of its people. Failure to turn to existing research for help concerning motivation, management, and human development is becoming costly. The inability to use what we know affects our schools, businesses, and culture far more than most Americans would like to believe. Not applying research findings in an organized, conscientious manner is a major part of the problem. The denial of the extreme importance of research establishes a foothold from which a demotivational element in America's institutions evolves. This demotivational element has a stranglehold on America's institutions. Its hidden effects must become visible to all.

The Great Missing Link

Research in human development has been progressing for years, but neglecting to make use of this research has become the great missing link in solving our problems.

Years ago, human behavior experts such as Sigmund Freud and Alfred Adler offered theories that some have now accepted as facts. These theories showed us the way to help people develop personalities and lifestyles that foster the enjoyment of life, work, play, and study. The benefits of these theories are well-researched, but some among us see to it that they are overlooked. Congress, CEOs, school administrators, parents, and government officials are just some of the expert spin doctors keeping us from using this valuable research.

Sigmund Freud, Alfred Adler, Harry Stack Sullivan, and Abraham Maslow all studied human development in terms of inspiration and motivation. The findings of these pioneers of psychology can foster understanding regarding the battle between lack of motivation and true productivity that has been brought on by poor management. Their findings can help bridge the gap between what we know about motivation and productivity, and what we apply. Misguided management can be reconsidered and reevaluated since man is the only animal capable of reevaluation.

Today, many psychologists, psychiatrists, psychoanalysts, educators, parents, and managers use traditional, trial-and-error, self-originated methods to get the best out of people. It is disturbing that basic principles of human development, known for decades, have become lost in the maze of new management techniques, motivational gimmicks, and fads in teaching and parenting.

Many basic principles have been neglected. Freud proved that early childhood experiences can affect development; that heredity plays a part, as do sexual and other emotional and psychological needs. He believed in his theory of psychoanalysis and the need for people to talk things out.

Freud and Adler, both famous contributors to the field of psychology, were very good friends until Adler decided that, even though Freud had contributed greatly to understanding human behavior, something was missing. Adler knew that certain needs, such as interaction with others and being accepted by fellow men and women, were important. He knew these needs had to be nourished if an individual was to be mentally healthy and productive. He believed that people are social beings born with natural inclinations to strive for achievement. He taught that people wanted to learn and seek meaning and fulfillment in their lives.

There is now evidence all around, significant clues and unobtrusive signs, that lend a great amount of support to Adler's theories of human development. Consider an area in which a large percentage of Americans spend time—the workplace. People often report on surveys and studies, and they behave in ways that also suggest that they want their work to provide the needs Adler believed in providing. A famous study done at Western Electric in Chicago as far back as 1927 revealed such findings. The University of Michigan has done several surveys that reveal people want to strive for achievement, seek meaning for themselves, and build self-esteem. Consulting firms have discovered that employees want a degree of self-governing, a feeling of importance, an interaction with colleagues, and an opportunity to be original and creative. Management in America's institutions must realize that, more than ever before, contented people work harder.

It seems to be an axiom of sorts that contented cows produce good milk and contented employees do good work. This axiom may become important to twenty-first century management.

Given this environment in the workplace, workers begin to interact, achieve acceptance, and find meaning and a sense of pride and success in their work. It is unfortunate, even approaching a state of urgency, that this is not happening in most American institutions and is not likely to change by the year 2000.

People want opportunities to do their best and to develop their skills and aptitudes. This will escalate as the twenty-first century approaches. It is sad that Adler's ideas have not been fully understood and accepted by government, business, and educational leaders. Little has been done to cultivate the science of human relationships.

This harmonious atmosphere desired by employees should be seen as a clue for management to identify the missing link between how people develop and how they become productive members of society.

Workers throughout America are crying out for recognition and gratification.

Basic to Adlerian psychology is the fact that discouragement is the basis for most misbehavior. Discouraged workers do not produce the best products, and discouraged students do not learn the things they are capable of learning. Discouraged teachers do not do their best job of teaching, and discouraged workers in many walks of life do not perform their duties or provide the services and products that others need.

Regarding motivational and human developmental problems in business, consider the words of Richard Pascale, who co-wrote *The Art of Japanese Management*.

> *A manager should be well enough developed as a human being to handle what a situation requires, not what the culture has taught him to be.*[1]

It is imperative to make certain in the immediate future that managers in America "are well enough developed" as human beings to handle "what a situation requires" and not interfere in the natural inclination to work and produce.

Pascale remarked, "One of the things I'm most powerfully moved by is the extraordinary hunger for social connectiveness among Americans that for many is not fulfilled by family or church . . . We spend an enormous percentage of our waking hours at work. That's where the muscle and mind goes, but the heart goes elsewhere."[1]

Our hearts are not going to work with us; and, as the saying goes, if our hearts are not in it, we will not do as well as we could.

It is clear that Pascale thinks that elements in a culture in which an individual is raised might well have an adverse effect on his or her development. America's culture has, almost invisibly, taught people how to demotivate and discourage each other. It is so common that it goes unseen. This unwanted teaching is a hidden force, so subconsciously ingrained into our culture that it is now depriving America of reaching its potential.

Managers are bosses, teachers, and parents; they are all responsible for the way people develop skills, acquire attitudes, and reach potential. Managers have many diverse personalities and can benefit from learning as much as possible about preventing lack of motivation through the use of an improved method of conversing and motivating. This can be done through learning basic human developmental skills.

These skills must be integrated into all American institutions in the years ahead if we are to become more adept at getting the best out of our people

Research, which we are neglecting, shows that failing to use these skills is costing our nation in terms of human development, motivation, and productivity. We are failing to defeat the unseen enemy.

Social connectiveness is still another clue to the missing link between a kinder, gentler, more encouraging form of managing and people who want to be encouraged to do their best. Harry Stack Sullivan, an American born in New York and schooled in Chicago, developed a sound interpersonal communication theory of personality development. His theory promotes the social connectiveness that Adler thought to be so important to development. Sullivan believed that people desired social connectiveness and interaction, and that they worked better where this type of environment was nurtured.

This theory is also part of the missing link between human development as it is being approached in American business and human development as it should be approached. If applied correctly, the theory would be more motivational for people. There is currently a smothering force, an attitude in the environment that stifles positive movement in people. This is our enemy. It is an attitude that has become a force, but it is unknown to most and is difficult to define. Yet it causes unwitting demotivation. It is difficult to define, yet it must be described in detail.

Sullivan believed that through personal interaction, people learn to behave in a particular way. He believed that people develop their own personality traits such as confidence or unsureness, constructive or destructive behavior, and pleasant or unpleasant attitudes and beliefs through conversations they have with people in their lives. Learning more facilitative ways to talk with each other would enable people to develop to a more satisfying degree and achieve at a higher level. Power-wielding, domineering attitudes that hinder good development would not be passed along.

Adler and Sullivan identified intricate aspects of human personality development that focused on human interaction. This focus on interaction has not been applied in businesses, schools, and families as it should be. The importance of interaction seemed to get lost and was not popular to use. The theory must now be considered as part of the missing link in human development.

Human interaction, using simple words and arranging them effectively, has more effect on how people develop than one would think. It would benefit our society to accept Adler and Sullivan's theories as fact. This would be a step forward in which American people could converse with each other in a more constructive, motivational way. Although it may seem simplistic, this idea of people learning to become more encouraging can root out the

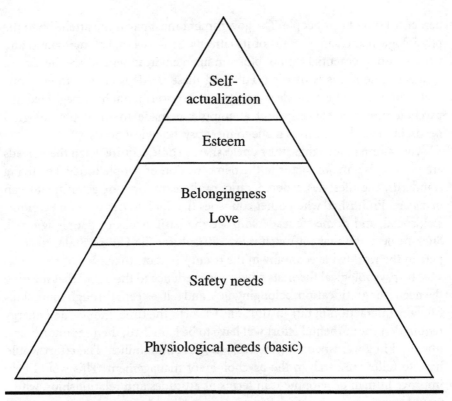

Figure 1.1   Maslow's heirarchy of needs.

smothering force, the unseen enemy, that is the culprit behind the motivational problems in America today. To eliminate this force would revitalize management and increase productivity.

Another famous theorist, Abraham Maslow, was a professor of psychology at Brandeis University. He believed that people have an active will toward health, an impulse toward growth or toward the actualization of human potential. Just like Adler and Sullivan, Maslow believed that these traits should not be extinguished or smothered by cultural misunderstandings about human development. Today America is basing much of its human development on these misunderstandings. It is becoming costly.

Maslow also developed a hierarchy of needs, as seen in Figure 1.1. Notice (at the bottom of the pyramid) that physiological and safety needs must be fulfilled first; then needs centering around belongingness, love, and self-esteem can be fulfilled. The system of government in America should effectively oversee all institutions, making sure these needs are being met in order to get the best effort out of our people. The government must pay more attention to the physiological and safety needs of its citizens. Self-esteem, belongingness, and working up to potential cannot blossom in an environment where the chance to meet these needs is missing. Fulfilling these needs is critical to everyone everywhere. It has become clear that leaders in government have neglected this psychological concept. Slipshod attempts are made to meet physiological needs, but even less effort is made to meet psychological needs.

The failure to recognize the hopelessness people acquire when these needs are not met is a major factor in the demotivation of people today. The living standards, the lifestyles a democratic, capitalistic form of government can bring are diminished when other countries that look to America for economical, social, and domestic leadership see the basic needs of people ignored. Such neglect will make it much more difficult for the United States to compete in the worldwide economy in the twenty-first century.

The psychological theorists have given credence to the belief that meeting the needs for gratification, belongingness, and self-esteem through more skillful daily interaction in our institutions is worth the time, money, and energy required. A monumental effort will have to be launched, then monitored and nurtured in government, businesses, schools, and families. The effort would have to follow research in the psychology of management. This would help improve human development in terms of attitudes and relationships, which would translate into better productivity in institutions.

American Management Has an Identity Crisis

Learning ways to bring the best out in people was not as important twenty-five years ago as it is now. It is unfortunate that old-fashioned discipline, such as President Reagan suggested, does not work as well as it did years ago in business and education. This change has occurred because of the emergence of worldwide communication systems. These universal communication systems brought vivid pictures of assassinations, wars, holocausts, hostage situations, terrorist actions, strikes, kidnappings, murders, and riots right into the living rooms of American homes. These events sent the message to old and young alike that to be free, independent, and self-governing, to be treated fairly with due process and in a humane way, was important as far as needs were concerned. It is sad because the great psychological theorists told us decades ago that these needs were important, and we have neglected them.

When President Reagan strongly hinted to the nation that we should return to old-fashioned discipline in our schools (and probably in the workplace), it was too late. Freedom of speech, the right to disagree and offer a dissenting view, and freedom of the press had been too well advertised.

These values, rights, and freedoms are constantly being discussed in the media and in the courts and classrooms. Democracy has, in effect, been advertised and sold about as well as Coke and Pepsi. Over forty thousand people climbed the Berlin wall before it was torn down to get to freedom. People hang off the edge of over-crowded boats and make other astounding efforts to reach our shores. Families have risked the lives of loved ones to save their relatives from autocratically governed countries. Illegal immigrants cross over our borders nightly.

In the 1950s and 1960s women said they wanted to be treated better. Students in America's colleges wanted to be better understood. Race riots plagued large cities. Black people marched in Alabama for rights they should have had without marching. It was a long walk to the back of the bus, and many black people took longer walks yet when they were not even allowed on a bus.

Bill Russell, perhaps the greatest man ever to play the center position in basketball, represented the United States in the Olympic games. He also won championships in NCAA competition and for the Boston Celtics in professional basketball. He recognized the inequities in society and why some people are not motivated, and he wrote about it in his book *Second Wind*. Russell declared,

---

For a country based on individual freedoms we sure are full of loopholes.[2]

Bill Russell verified this viewpoint when he visited the Basketball Hall of Fame and found out that his Celtic uniform had been placed on a white mannequin! Maslow tried to tell us that belongingness, recognition, social connectiveness, and self-esteem are all individual needs that a country must carefully nurture if it is to motivate its people. We cannot afford loopholes that affect freedoms, but many still exist.

America has an identity crisis. It is not changing as fast as evolving countries should. It is hiding and running away from its duty to guarantee individual freedoms. Few leaders have indicated they see that the erosion of these freedoms causes the tension that invites the drugs and increases violence. The political parties continue to find figures that relay the message that things are getting better. Of course, this means that the needs of more Americans are being met. Since violence, poverty, health care, and education are the main issues in elections, one can surmise that things are not getting better for the vast majority of Americans. Citizens of the United States are more fearful about their jobs than ever before; more are homeless, without health coverage, pensions, and access to education. Fear of being a victim of a crime is worse now than ever. America cannot survive another century if violence continues to increase.

America is still the most democratic country in the world, but prejudices as well as autocratic, old-fashioned methods of motivation are still practiced. This results in America not being as democratic as the rest of the world perceives us. Many businesses and schools are clinging to autocratic systems of managing and developing people. Unwanted tension is created when people feel their individual freedoms are being eroded and the American dream has become elusive to them.

The identity crisis stems from the fact that government keeps saying things are getting better when the people know they are getting worse. Insecurity promotes fear. When there is insecurity in the workplace and ineffective motivation in our schools, there will be tension in homes. When these ills arise in a society, the basic physiological needs of people are often not met; the attention to safety is diminished. Psychological needs suffer as people think less of themselves and of their ability to provide for each other. As this condition explodes, the tension spills over into streets.

The might-is-right, top-down style of management is strangling the nation. The inability to recognize this archaic approach to good human development is becoming more and more costly each year. The top-down management approach is at the root of today's productivity and motivational problems as well as the identity crisis the country is suffering. Erroneous attitudes and old-fashioned, autocratic methods of motivation are undermining the natural desire of people to achieve for their own satisfaction. To allow them to do so would fulfill the needs that the autocratic system denies exist. By providing an atmosphere in businesses, schools, and homes where physiological as well as psychological needs are met, we would cut violence considerably. The government drastically underestimates the role of psychological needs in the laws and policies handed down through an autocratic system. It adds to the identity crisis instead of helping to eliminate it.

Many people, particularly the young, whose needs are not being met try to satisfy their natural inclinations to be independent. They send signals through their behavior that should be heeded by our society. In order to escape from the autocratic, traditional environment, they seek what, to them, is a better existence by using drugs and alcohol or by just running away. They rebel in many ways against an environment at school, work, or at home that is only cosmetically democratic.

Part of the identity crisis in which America finds itself as we head into the twenty-first century is the government's casual approach to changing what has become an autocratic environment. Young people rebel against such environments, and employees often try to as well, even though most are defeated. Such environments stifle energy and enthusiasm, and they set up a situation where people, especially youth, become dependent on those telling them what to do every minute of the day. This environment directly conflicts with the information the great theorists in psychology suggested for us. They agreed that institutions should be places where encouragement and inspiration prevail and bring about satisfaction and high productivity.

It is unfortunate that many of our institutions are organized in such a way that people want to escape from them. It is even more unfortunate that the government allows an imbalance of power to be in charge of institutions. In the 1980s and 1990s, it has been incorrectly perceived by the government and the courts that if management cannot control everything from behavior to productivity, then things will collapse. Managing in the twenty-first century will have to include more non-management input on decisions that have impact on workers. This concept is more likely to meet needs, eliminate tension, and provide stability to any twenty-first century organization. The identity crisis arises because we are not ready to take the risk of allowing input from those who suffer the effects of autocratic, top-down management. Such thinking will need to be revised in managing people in the twenty-first century.

A Nation at Risk or Just in Transition?

A Nation at Risk, the report researched in the 1980s by the federal government in an attempt to upgrade education, revealed that our young people were not grasping important courses, such as math and science. The report suggested America could be at risk because we would not be able to move forward as quickly as other countries in the field of technology, and therefore would not be able to compete in the international markets.

The at-risk factor could mean the nation would not have the ability in the future to create a sound defense system. Our system might not compare favorably to those of other countries whose educational systems have the ability to help their young people grasp math and science necessary for the year 2000 and beyond.

In essence, *A Nation at Risk* did not apply just to education; it revealed that we are not developing people in all of our institutions to the extent that may be needed. This means that somewhere in the future, the skills and knowledge needed by Americans to keep the society dynamic will be missing. This reaches beyond math and science. Experts in economics, ecology, health, agriculture, business, education, automation, and many other fields so much needed for a society to function may not be available.

A nation deeply rooted in traditional methods of human development does not make rapid changes and does not want to relinquish what has made it comfortable in the past. Efforts in the United States have usually kept it ahead of the rest of the world in regard to education, but times have changed. Business and education have been slow to make appropriate adjustments, and this now plagues effectiveness.

The nation will be at risk in the future unless people in our institutions learn to connect and interact socially with each other in an honest, harmonious way. Managing in the twenty-first century will mean identifying elements that can improve daily interaction between people. Learning how to identify and implement these elements is a major step in eliminating the label, a nation at risk. It will help overcome traditional but ineffective methods of motivation and human development, and will increase productivity.

Perhaps the country is not at risk. Perhaps it is only in transition, undergoing stress and change. If this is so, it is of paramount importance that we identify and change those elements that are having an effect on today's problems of motivation. We should be aware that social interaction and its dynamics are strongly connected to this problem. Making changes here would help make the transition from the industrial society of the 1960s, 1970s, and 1980s to the information society in the twenty-first century.

Managing in the twenty-first century will mean restructuring and reengineering, but not in the way being done now. It will allow more people to participate, to have a greater voice and to share in nearly every aspect of any institution, whether it be in business or education.

Current autocratic attitudes and traditional beliefs culturally ingrained in government, business, and educational officials may hinder this restructuring. These autocratic attitudes are the obscure, hidden forces behind the misguided motivation we are seeing in American institutions today. These leaders and decision makers often have mistaken philosophies of how to get the best effort out of people. They are not psychologically sound philosophies.

They do not bring employees into solutions, something which is needed to provide them with gratification, recognition, and a sense of security. These philosophies, based on external motivation, undermine psychological needs.

It is obvious that a true participatory democracy, one psychologically sound, would help meet the needs Maslow described, especially that of belongingness. If interactions can be improved so people can understand each other better, as Harry Stack Sullivan suggested, basic needs such as self-esteem, gratification from work, recognition, and belongingness can be promoted to a higher degree. Loyalty could return to the workplace and not be a lost virtue.

One of the problems of today's motivation in America was mentioned by John Naisbitt in the book *Megatrends.*

In the United States, there is a fundamental mismatch between traditional American love of personal liberty and the top-down, authoritarian manner in which the American workplace has operated. Employees habitually surrender the most basic rights, free speech and due process, for example, when at work each day.[3]

The phrase "American love of personal liberty" should be considered part of the neglected research in American management. Optimum productivity cannot occur when management gives off the impression that personal liberties will be treated lightly. Adler's theory that man will strive to do well if treated fairly and given a reasonable opportunity is applicable here.

"Authoritarian manner" stifles the energy it professes to bring out, energy that is so important for America to unleash now. Authority versus liberty is the "fundamental mismatch" that John Naisbitt mentioned in *Megatrends* (published in 1982). He tried to write a futuristic book, one that might predict things to come as America moved into the twenty-first century. We could benefit from accepting his view about authority versus liberty as the "fundamental mismatch" in our society as we head into the next century.

Many Americans see the abuse of authority that leads to the denial of individual freedoms as an America that is becoming less sensitive to the Constitution and the freedoms it promised to deliver. The insensitive America that is developing ensures more violence and chaos in the country. A country that becomes callous and insensitive to the needs and rights of its people will never live up to the expectations and the hope that the people within the country have built up.

Even though America is the most democratic country in the world, it is clear that it is not as democratic as it could be or even was at one time. By becoming more democratic in its institutions, America could be more effective for its people and as a world power.

It seems we have forgotten that democracy means government of, by, and for the people.

As global competition increases in the twenty-first century, America cannot afford to have employee rights, for example, approached as casually as they were in the 1970s, 1980s, and 1990s. David Ewing, an editor at the *Harvard Business Review* and an outspoken advocate of employee rights, said the average American worker is "nearly rightless . . . 9:00 a.m. until 5:00 p.m., Monday through Friday."[4]

Furthermore, traditional American management has adopted an insulting top-down approach to a worker's knowledge in his or her own job. Managers in the United States have consistently denied workers the opportunity to make substantive decisions about how their jobs should be done. Only now are we beginning to see that this elitist strategy has cost America top honors in world productivity growth.[3]

Management practices in the educational system will not change rapidly because business dictates management style in this country. It is sad that the one great hope for educational reform in the next century is linked to what course business management follows. We must hope that business will see management as more of a participatory process than it does now. With that participation comes the social connectiveness, interaction, and encouragement that our schools so much need to copy. The authoritarian manner and elitist, top-down approach to getting the best effort out of people is the number one problem America's institutions face as we enter the twenty-first century.

Most states still have a fire-at-will law on the books, which means people can be fired for any reason. But they are often fired for speaking out, being too old, being the wrong color, or not favoring the sexual advances of the boss. The government has given lip service to the idea that employees can even be lied about in the workplace, and if the untruths are kept in the workplace, the worker is almost legally helpless to defend himself or herself.

Many companies, such as Quality of Work Life, were given lip service in the 1970s and 1980s, then died out in the 1990s as reengineering, restructuring, and downsizing covered up most forms of discrimination. There have not been any real attempts to help businesses make the transition from being authoritarian to participatory, and that lack will keep America at risk as it enters the next century.

Courage to Change

Management in the twenty-first century must have the courage to make drastic changes. This will be crucial if the nation is going to make an effort to change itself into world leader regarding psychological aspects of the workplace and if it is going to improve human development and motivational techniques. Of course, becoming the world leader in these aspects of society would give the United States an advantage in many areas. To neglect doing this as we have done in the past only places us at the mercy of other countries that may soon see the need and muster the courage to implement such need-providing human development.

Human resource technology, not automobile, radio, television, or computer technology, is the technology in which the nation is at risk. We are at risk if we do not have the courage to try something different, something based on research that will fulfill needs and thereby motivate people to be more productive. Productivity is the major element that creates living standards in a capitalistic society. When productivity declines, living standards decline.

At one time business did show some courage in trying to change the way it operated. Many companies developed human resource development departments, but as is customary by top-down management, they were not allowed to be effective in initiating participation of the workforce. No behavior change in the top-down approach took place and, as a result, no attitude change in employees occurred either. Human resources would be a good place to start reorganization into a more participatory model between labor and management if only top management would understand the benefits of such a model. As of now, human resource departments are usually just holding the status quo in the top-down approach.

Signals received from people in institutions that self-reliance and initiative is waning must be recognized sooner and, in a method to be described here, eradicated effectively. Effectively is a key word because many attempts are made in organizations to restore energy, enthusiasm, and spirit, but most fizzle out over time because the misguided motivational techniques of top management prevail. In order to bring about this needed change, leaders in government and business will have to muster enough courage to change some of their long-held beliefs, attitudes, prejudices, and values if they want to create an environment that brings the best out in people.

In the early 1980s a book titled *In Search of Excellence* was published. It revealed to a delicate point the things that good institutions do to earn the title "good." The research in it has been neglected, and an attempt will be made here to show how the business world neglect of research will haunt us well into the twenty-first century if drastic reorganization is not undertaken soon. Following is one insight borrowed from *In Search of Excellence*[5] that describes America's business climate in the 1980s and 1990s and why it must change.

Analytic Ivory Towers

The reason behind the absence of focus on product or people in so many American companies, it would seem, is the simple presence of a focus on something else. That something else is over-reliance on analysis from corporate ivory towers and over-reliance on financial sleight of hand, the tools that would appear to eliminate risk, but also, unfortunately, eliminate action.[5]

Over-reliance on analysis from corporate ivory towers promotes distrust. It certainly does not meet needs for gratification and self-reliance about which the great psychologists informed us. Over-reliance on management's judgment is the essence of top-down management. It is a large component of today's lack of motivation in the workplace. This over-reliance makes the employees feel that their input concerning ways to improve the company does not count with management. Over a period of time, workers feel that basic needs such as being secure and gratified at work are unmet. Over-reliance on analysis from the ivory tower is a direct contradiction to the needs ladder taught to us by psychologist Abraham Maslow.

Shareholders, CEOs, and board members have shunned the importance of psychology in the business world. This fact is shown throughout this book. Leaders in good, psychologically sound companies and other organizations know there are no wrong ideas, and they can respond to employee suggestions in such a way that the employee knows that his ideas were considered, that his thoughts and feelings and interests were shared even if his idea was not implemented.

Even the word *worker* can promote distance between employees and management, and distance is the catalyst for the development of distrust. In the near future, courage on the part of management will be needed to remove distance so it can promote trust and increase productivity. Research is telling us that eliminating distance between management and labor will promote belongingness and security, and will increase productivity. When people believe they are being productive and helping a company or organization, their self-esteem blossoms.

Not only does over-reliance on ivory towers promote distrust, it promotes dependence. One executive reiterated that he thinks many managers, in their autocratic styles, continually tell people what to do and then complain that these people cannot do anything for themselves. These traditional managers create dependence on their ideas as to how things should be done. Employees just wait for guidance from the ivory tower positions before doing anything. They are not inspired to do anything that might help change the company for the better. They have been sapped of their spirit, and over-reliance on analysis from the top has been the most dominant factor.

Future management will have to develop ways to provide meaning for people as they work each day. Providing meaning fits in with supplying the basic psychological needs that are badly missing in America's workplaces. Meaning in a job means productivity in that job.

As this book is being written, there is a fundamental disagreement between what labor believes is needed to keep America vibrant and what top-down management believes. A few government officials seem to understand the problem, but businesses that donate huge funds to political parties keep undermining change efforts. As a result, workers are still demotivated by traditional, nonresearch-based methods. Secretary of Labor in the Clinton administration, Robert Reich, may have said it best regarding how the American worker should be treated:

> *There are those who treat workers as assets to be developed while others treat workers as costs to be cut.*[6]

On the other side, many CEOs, shareholders, and corporate board members maintain that the psychological well-being of employees should not even be considered in the profit-driven business world.

In the twenty-first century, government for the people and by the people could be on a collision course with a business world that turns its nose up at the needs of people who work hard to make the businesses competitive in local and global markets. It is going to take a tremendous amount of soul-searching and courage for business leaders and lawmakers with top-down, ivory-tower attitudes to change their thinking if America is to remain competitive.

It is unfortunate that currently we have so many companies, schools, and homes that are incapable of providing meaning because research-based human development and motivational skills are missing. The top-down approach to motivation is running roughshod over people, and the sooner we can change it, the better.

It is a sad situation when top-down, authoritarian management knows, at least to a small degree, that it is important to create a climate conducive to productivity, then uses destructive methods to create it. It is difficult for anyone needing to get the best out of someone else to overcome that which the culture has taught him is the best way to get results from this person. Often, because of cultural tradition, management will tear down the worker, although it is not intended. The manager is unaware of the effects of his words or actions. Such tyranny is not intended, but it is happening far too often in America's workplaces. Most organizations do not plan to deprive people of fulfillment of their needs, they just are. It is an unseen enemy that affects our ability to get the best out of our people.

This unseen force prevents America from meeting the needs of many people. These needs need to be met in order for the country to be safe, free of fear, and one that creates opportunity for many who are willing and able to work. The needs the great psychologists told us about cannot be fulfilled in American institutions as they are organized today, in businesses or in schools. That is because the negative view of people, which promotes verbal beratement, is commonplace.

Management of the future will have to understand better how to build up, not tear down, the self-images of workers in order to ensure optimal development and optimal productivity.

Ingrained in top-down management is the fact that American management has *learned*, yes learned, to dismember self-esteem in others. It is an unintended, ingrained, demotivational force rampaging through the country. In our society, people are approached as being unable rather than able. Many people who accomplished great things were told they would never amount to much. Taking a negative view of people is not new. It is unfortunate that this cultural trait has promoted over-reliance on the ivory-tower style of management. It should not be so difficult for us to see how we approach people as being unable, but it is because the concept has been with us so long. We tend to believe that something so well-accepted does not need to be changed, and we just continue to teach it by example.

Courage is taking a stand in the face of opposition, or facing danger or trying to overcome adversity. It is sadly lacking in those who have the power to make changes for the better in America's institutions. Government, business, and education officials do not want to step forward to bring about change even though today's problem of motivating workers and students is discussed often in the media. Bosses continue to sap the spirit of employees. No one willingly wants to participate in this discouraging demise, yet no one stops it.

The ingredients for change, then, are that people recognize the unintentional, traditional, top-down style of management, see that a change in this style is morally correct, then take a stand even if some form of opposition might come their way. Because these demotivating forces promote slow sabotage instead of a sudden strike, it is easier to hold onto them. We keep repeating the sabotage because the forces are hidden to us. We must overcome holding the status quo on demotivation just as assuredly as we have overcome other crises.

The courage to change the way we develop our people should not come from an external stimulus, such as the attack on Pearl Harbor or another depression. Americans, especially those in leadership positions, must become internally motivated to make these changes. The best athletes and the best students are internally motivated. Those in charge of correcting things in the United States should develop internal courage to do something about our motivational and human development problems.

Beyond a Shadow of a Doubt

Up to this point, we have shown how research in human development, business psychology, and leadership has been neglected. The basic needs of human beings must be met in American institutions if America is to remain competitive in the twenty-first century. It has been mentioned that successful businesses, schools, and families understand how to satisfy these vital ingredients and get the best out of their members. This subtle factor will be explained in detail as the unseen enemy of today's problems of motivation and productivity are pursued and clearly identified.

Beyond a shadow of a doubt, the alienation, resentment, and lack of trust in management techniques in the 1980s and 1990s have spread discontentment, discouragement, and a lack of loyalty, resembling a rampaging wildfire running through the world of management. Such a business climate evolves when leaders are not trained to recognize how they kill the spirit of workers.

Americans must do all they can to organize a more cooperative system of work designed to get the best out of each other. It will need to be more systematic and more scientific. A good starting place might be the federal, state, and local governments, where a new system would involve fairer and quicker methods of resolving disputes that cost production time. Top government officials will have to take the lead in this enormous task. Few have done so up to the present time because businesses using top-down management contribute money to most of our elected officials to gain favors. As a result, people's faith in government is declining.

In the twenty-first century, it will be imperative for government, labor, and business to work together to introduce legislation that will provide incentives and programs to help change attitudes within America's institutions, programs designed to promote a kinder, more motivational, and inspirational governing of people.

The United States government cannot come across to the American people as being dedicated to forming a more effective, more perfect union if it does not strive to change the insensitive, discouraging approach it currently clings to in developing and motivating its people.

Safe food, clean water, and affordable, secure housing and goods used every day by citizens are essential to any society that is to remain strong within. The biggest challenge for those elected in governing the country in the future will be bringing about drastic change in the top-down management style that grips the nation and hinders optimal fulfillment of these necessities. The enemy within is causing America to become more tense now than during any other time in its history.

Reform of the top-down approach will involve using less power and force over people in the managing process. While the country struggles to remain competitive in business, industry, and education, it would be irresponsible, as is our custom, to apply more pressure to get results. Such irresponsibility will cause working and learning environments to become even more tense in the future. These environments will meet fewer needs as superiors expect and try to get more. In business, it is the bottom line. In education, it is accountability. But the opposite is true: the more need-filling management becomes, the more productivity it might expect to get.

Subtle changes in our society have made it more difficult for the United States worker to be motivated by fear, humiliation, or expendability. Union contracts have diminished some of the fear, and the judicial system has helped as well; but the nation could benefit from a system that does not need such radical final verdicts. Big business, for example, should not force Congress to search for ways and means to meet the economic needs of people. It should, to show it cares about employees, search for these ways and means itself. But that attitude is not prevalent in most businesses today. For example, business should be able to figure out what a good wage is and not have the government decide a minimum wage for it. However, a sense of fairness is not usually included in the unregulated code of conduct of those at the top in corporate America.

Since psychological needs of workers have become more important in our fast-paced society, workers silently say to themselves that the employer "must pay me for the right to make me miserable. I was born seeking freedom, independence, meaning, recognition, gratification, and growth." Companies that deny psychological needs must realize that this is a major reason behind strikes and the lack of optimal, unforced productivity and the settling of contracts. It is a factor behind companies declaring bankruptcy and having to downsize. The media reporting on strikes or near strikes seldom mentions psychological needs as an issue because benefits and pay raises are usually at the forefront.

The entire process of top-down management causes those *in charge* to get upset with the *troops*, who are forced to create a balance between criticism and their own self-esteem or, put another way, they do what they have to do to feel reasonably good about themselves. They try not to express the emotions they feel daily when their psychological needs are not met while they work in the trenches.

In regard to the relationship between labor and management in the United States, each side is sure the other is at fault when the business is not prospering. Management sees labor in a negative way, as being lazy and unproductive.

Labor sees management as autocratic, domineering, and psychologically bankrupt. Neither side is capable of seeing how resentment builds up because needs are not fulfilled. It must be considered that not feeling good psychologically about oneself will probably cause some physiological ailment in the future. Companies often end up paying not only for the psychological needs the autocratic process denies, but also for the more costly physiological needs as well.

Time often means productivity. Time is lost through having to work out problems in the workplace caused by neglecting the research that could have prevented the time loss. Plus, that time could have been spent doing things to keep the business humming. As will be discovered in the pages ahead, avoiding research that could have helped in keeping disputes to a minimum has become costly to the United States. In many cases, this lost productivity could have prevented companies from laying off people and losing customer confidence.

Management techniques designed not to get in the way of meeting the needs of people who want to work are techniques that can be installed almost immediately. Technical know-how was not the major reason Japanese workers, during Japan's resurgence, were able to produce nearly twice as many cars in a year as the American workers. Motivation was a factor. The autocratic, top-down approach causes workers in America to withdraw their energy. Often the energy has to go into fighting court battles or union grievances just to quell friction between people. Promises of lifetime employment, which are a form of a security (fulfilling a need), helped Japan's production early in its resurgence.

Trust, Diplomacy, Honesty, and Integrity

Trust is the underlying principle needed to implement a systematic approach to providing human needs in the American workplace. Trust promotes confidence, courage, spirit, inspiration, and energy. Its absence causes deterioration. It is the most important factor in an attempt to get the best out of people. In a society based on healthy competition, differing viewpoints will, if things are working well, evolve often. Diplomacy, which is usually based in honesty and integrity, should prevail if the differing viewpoints are to be worked out.

An agreement made through democratic procedures and fair to both sides will take longer, but the chaos and stress currently devastating motivation in the workplace in America can be prevented by not relying on the old-fashioned, autocratic, top-down approach.

If people believe that America is at a position in the world where its reputation is becoming eroded, they can blame the erosion on the lack of trust currently expanding in the workplace. The distrust between employer and employee, and how this scorpion of suspicion works its way under the skin of a society, is possibly the most devastating element in conquering today's problems of lack of motivation. It must be confronted by all leaders in all institutions, especially government and business, if America is to become a more inspirational, less tense, more productive country in the twenty-first century.

Distrust drains the vital energy and excitement that Adler and others so expertly identified within people. Without trust, the spirit of competition is thwarted, and people become at risk with each other. Although it may not be looked upon as part of the neglected research being discussed, Karl Marx, of all people, may have had a view about capitalism distrust that we should consider as we try to make changes in our culture. William G. Ouchi notes this in *Theory Z:*

> Karl Marx foresaw this distrust as the inevitable product of capitalism
> and the force that, in his view, would bring about the ultimate failure of
> capitalism.[7]

Karl Marx's concept of government, namely communism, finally devastated Russia. Disillusionment promoted by autocratic distrust flourished more than Marx realized in the Soviet Union and brought about its ultimate decline. This demise should be a clue to all other countries that distrust is a major factor they should eliminate. In communist institutions, Marx proclaimed that there was little distrust to cause problems in productivity. This enemy of motivation was hidden to Marx, just as the effects of distrust are hidden to leaders in America. It can be unrecognizable until it is too late.

There are organizations that try hard to expose the distrust. Solidarity, the union of people in Poland, tried to expose distrust. State human rights departments and the Federal Equal Employment Opportunity Commission are government agencies that have the authority to stop discrimination, retaliation, harassment, and other forms of distrust in the workplace. It is discouraging that investigations by Congress reveal that these agencies have not championed the rights of enough citizens and have not given Americans the broadest protection available in a democracy. The government's casual

---

[7] W. Ouchi, *Theory Z*, (page 5) © 1981 by Addison Wesley Publishing Company, Inc. Reprinted by permission of Addison Wesley Longman.

approach toward eliminating distrust is perhaps the number one problem throughout America today.

Distrust flourishes because the autocratic, top-down approach to motivation and managing is so deeply entrenched in American culture that it is difficult for elected officials to see the devastating effect it has on the entire country.

The ultimate failure that Karl Marx predicted for the United States may not be very close since the failure of the Soviet Union put it at military and economical disadvantages. The Soviet Union failure came from forces within. This internal force is the exact force the United States must guard against. It can do so by paying attention to how it is developing its people. The Soviet Union had a rather severe case of the top-down approach. Its government was not able to create an environment in which the needs of people were being met by what they produced.

America has the opportunity to control its own destiny because it has been able to observe firsthand what the distrustful enemy did to the Soviet Union. Russian leaders must wonder why the oppressive, top-down approach to managing is not very need-satisfying for their people. Fear, such as was used in Russia, is a motivator as candy can be to a child, but both are *external* motivators. They are temporary. America must do the exact opposite of what the Soviet Union autocracy did. It must strive to create an environment that promotes self-motivation—the best kind of motivation. But it can be extinguished rather quickly with poor human development techniques disguised as being inspirational and motivational.

Institutions, organizations, governments, classrooms, and homes that are organized around fear and expendability as a primary force for meaningful movement of people are doomed to fail. Motivation based on fear takes too much time to monitor because fear takes so much out of the human species. When the fear peddlers are not around, people take an emotional break to get in touch with themselves. Many managers and a multitude of American teachers and parents base their ideas of getting the best out of people on similar false assumptions. This was seen in the oppressive fear used to develop people in the Soviet Union. Fear *demotivates*. It affects *future energy*.

People in the Soviet Union ran out of energy to work within a government that was not providing needs. Make no mistake about it, these needs were both physiological and psychological. A motivational force other than fear is needed in the United States in order to create a more reliable, consistent, and permanent development of people.

Maslow's theory about meeting needs should now be universally accepted in order to bring about this motivational force. Adler's theory that man is a social being seeking meaning should also be accepted, understood, and implemented. These theories, which should be considered as part of the neglected research, are important for all human beings to understand each other much more thoroughly. This better understanding is needed to keep spirits high. Otherwise, trust breaks down, alienation occurs, suspicion overwhelms, and the vitality sought in people dissipates.

Trust at high levels in organizations can promote and maintain movement, meaningful movement, in people. John Gardner in his book *Morale* profoundly observed,[8]

Man is a stubborn seeker of meaning.[8]

These words would fit perfectly into Adler's thinking. Consider how often do American workers say, "I just do what they tell me to do." This American worker is not creating, producing, or originating as he or she should be. For workers to "just do what they tell me to do" will be devastating to the United States in the twenty-first century.

Of course, making changes to get the best out of people does not just include motivating people in businesses and schools. It includes motivating people to stop actions such as gang violence, murder, rape, child abuse, dishonesty in influential offices, and other acts against people in our society. Institutional changes described here will curtail the unfair treatment of women, young people, the aged, the handicapped, and those who speak out, and will bring down racial barriers that still flourish in the United States.

President Franklin D. Roosevelt was right on target when he told the country that if our civilization is to survive, we must cultivate the science of human relationships. It is a science that must become better understood, especially by those in any type of leadership position. It is up to leaders of the future to refine, then pass on this science to generations ahead. Research has shown us that it is now possible to determine how relationships break down. This can be done in a much more scientific and systematic manner than ever before.

Human relations experts now know the once-invisible elements that tore down relationships when no one knew why. There are ways to teach people how to change attitudes about how people best develop. Power, for example, is abused in most relationships that break down. This is true whether we are talking about divorce or a management and labor issue. It is true when we discuss problems between teacher and student or parent and child.

Cultivating the science of human relationships involves intricate study of pet American-born phrases uttered every day that are demotivational in content, but are not recognized as such. Learning how to eliminate sarcasm, belittlement, ridicule, embarrassment, humiliation, and other popular but dead wrong forms of motivation can now be so exact that the process can be called scientific. If not scientific, as President Roosevelt said, the process can be much more systematic.

Research informs us that the language spoken in businesses, schools, and homes is far more demotivational than we would ever imagine. Using words in a different way is part of the process, but the primary focus must be on changing ingrained attitudes that cause people to use the words that cause relationships to fall apart.

An attitude change about how best to get people to do things must come before people can realize how to arrange the words differently. The words flow better once an individual is able to change from a top-down, power-laden attitude to a more encouraging, inspirational attitude. The rest of the book will be dedicated to changing the prevalent top-down attitude so devastating in America today. Examples will be given, and it is hoped that the reader will have a better understanding as to how the top-down, power-oriented approach to developing people is not only America's unseen enemy within, but is the world's enemy within.

A continued insensitive attitude by the government and those who manage others will continue to promote the smothering force in our society that makes people say they do not like the way they are being governed and managed.

Good management and good motivation are the exceptions and not the rules in America today. We should make them the rules.

This enrichment process must be organized around the idea that what is currently known about getting the best out of people must be more readily applied in businesses, schools, and homes. Psychological and physiological needs must be met, but met through a restructuring of how people are managed.

America and its wealth can no longer afford to buy off the unfulfilled needs that Adler and Maslow maintained are so important. Theory must be put into practice by focusing on ways to change attitudes and, through deep introspection into our culture, understand more thoroughly what people do to each other to cause feelings of discouragement, disenchantment, distrust, and suspicion. Promoting harmony should be easier.

Utopia is not possible even in the twenty-first century, but a more harmonious, productive America is possible. The demise of the U.S.S.R., with Japan now hitting a plateau, gives us a second chance to restructure our society into a more humane, productive one.

Theory must be put into practice by focusing on measurable ways to meet needs and eliminate traditional attitudes. It will take a great deal of internal vigilance as well as uncommon, bipartisan legislation by government and business leaders to make such a commitment. The changes will have to be monitored with a great deal of scrutiny and zeal. We may have enough laws on the books now, such as those regarding labor relations, age, sex, and race discrimination, but they are not enforced with any amount of zeal. Government and business do not see the tension and stress created by the lack of monitoring. Optimal productivity is not possible in such environments.

The leaders taking part in this needs-initiative drive will thus be using the facilitative management skills that research has given us—skills we have neglected. Instead of top-down management neglecting the research, it will be setting a good example and ridding itself of the autocratic, tension-filled approach that affects productivity and motivation in today's America. The America of tomorrow can be better.

As we look to the twenty-first century and consider the effects neglected research has had on management and human development, it might be wise to consider the words of former President John F. Kennedy:

An error does not become a mistake until you refuse to correct it.[9]

2 | The Spirit Killers

Introduction

The research being neglected in business and management and organizational psychology reaches as far back as 1927. However, avoiding the more recent research done in the early 1980s by Peters and Waterman in their book *In Search of Excellence* has also cost business plenty. In the book, Peters and Waterman noted two important things that have been overlooked in the good companies in the United States:

> A true people orientation can't exist unless there is a special language to go with it.[9]

Few if any companies have implemented a "special language." Most management teams would say it is just a fad so they can maintain the devastating top-down approach. Such a stance prohibits top-level productivity. It kills the spirit of employees.

The second important thing mentioned by Peters and Waterman in *In Search of Excellence* was, "The larger context of high performance, we believe, is intrinsic motivation."[9] It is from this quote that we can see it was reported many years ago that to improve the way people talk to each other might instill the intrinsic motivation needed in all organizations.

Businesses, schools, and most families in America base their motivation on external rather than internal or intrinsic motivation. This erroneous attitude, as the great psychologists have tried to tell us, is becoming more and more costly the longer we cling to it.

Leaders who have painfully tried to point us in the right direction have focused on the idea that more sophistication is needed in managing and motivating people.

These leaders stressed that relationship-building should become more of a science.

Although it can never become an exact science, it can become more systematic in our institutions. It can become a craft. The devastating effects of the top-down style of management can be monitored and diminished in almost any institution by implementing a new, more encouraging language.

In order to bring about this systematic method of human development, the ineffective methods that cultural tradition has led management to accept must be better understood. Once understood, more refined methods of motivation can be built into institutions. Results will show an increase in productivity and learning from those institutions that are courageous enough to attempt change. In time, this systematic approach becomes less and less systematic as it becomes part of the institution's internal mode of operation

America has within it far too many people who could be performing at a higher level. They are frustrated because of the nearly forced acceptance of top-down management that is smothering and limiting their production. America is suffering from within because of a spirit-killing force that is an integral part of the elitist, top-down form of managing people. If we cannot find a way to change this currently unrecognized spirit-killing force, sometime in the twenty-first century America could suffer the worst set back in its history.

America must survive the violent, greedy, apathetic, need-depriving society we have created. We need to get back to the attitudes that made America strong in the first place. We need loyalty between employer and employee, where both take pride in the success of an institution whether it be big or small. We need an atmosphere where people can socially connect with each other in the business world and other organizations.

A work environment centered around improved language that allows intrinsic motivation to flourish would eliminate the climate of fear and abuse of power currently playing on the minds of most American workers each day. Layoffs are mentioned daily in newspapers or on television, and many think, *I wonder if it could happen to me.* In the 1990s, major companies laid off 10,000 people or more. They were well-known, trusted companies such as IBM, Motorola, AT&T, Ford, Boeing, General Motors, and Sears.

American institutions have boxed themselves into an atmosphere where distrust, ridicule, resentment, retaliation, alienation, harassment, deceit, discontent, humiliation, stress, tension, fear, and embarrassment breed and feed. These common spirit-killing elements do not produce strength, do not promote social connection and gratification, do not provide recognition or any of the other needs psychologists note we need. These elements do not promote harmony and cooperation and loyalty that all institutions need. Instead, they promote tension that needs to be released.

The tension created by the culturally transmitted ingredients listed above is not completely apparent to America's politicians, executives, and corporate board of directors. This misunderstanding explains why there is so little being done to eradicate the tension that brings about the violence, homelessness, declining education, and other maladies in our society.

Those who will be responsible for leading others in the twenty-first century must be well enough trained in human relations and motivation to avoid the culturally transmitted over-reliance on the top-down approach. They must be able to promote meaningful social interaction and intrinsic motivation by learning and then speaking a more encouraging language. This will eliminate the spirit killers from feeding in institutions.

Incorporating such change into America's power-oriented companies will not be easy. Some research studies indicate that even those people who have received training in management, psychology, human development, personality and learning theory, counseling techniques, and therapy are not very helpful. They are not far enough along as human development experts to help institutions recognize and eradicate the spirit killers. They are not able to bring about the change needed to create a more harmonious atmosphere. They are, according to the research, *ordinary men* when assessed as to their ability to help people develop.[10]

Ordinary men will not be able to deal with the extraordinary problems the twenty-first century brings to America's business world, education, and the family makeup. We cannot afford to have ordinary men as our politicians, managers, board directors, teachers, coaches, counselors, priests, and others we now call leaders. We must skillfully redevelop them or others to become adept at organizing our institutions in the twenty-first century.

Our culture teaches too many things that focus on using power over people, and such authoritarian leadership is killing the spirit of too many Americans.

The development of leaders was touched upon by Richard Pascale when he discussed how managers should be developed. Pascale stated that, "A manager should be well enough developed as a human being to handle what a situation requires, not what the culture has taught him to be."[11]

Spirit killing is so much a part of our culture that few people can recognize the exact event or just how the spirit of a person begins to tail off into an "I don't care" attitude. Discouragement is so commonplace in our society that we are not very adept at recognizing those elements that cause it. Of course, this just compounds the problem of trying to make institutions more harmonious and productive. Top management of today has deceived itself into believing that harmony is not necessary for productivity. Late twentieth-century management has neglected the psychology of human development to the extent that they want employees to put emotions behind them. There is no way to arrive at optimal output with this approach.

Today, American management believes that it is no longer responsible for the morale of employees. That is like saying parents are no longer a force behind the constructive or destructive movement of a child. It is like a coach claiming he does not have responsibility to motivate his team.

Those who aspire to lead must understand that they are responsible for improving the present and the *future energy* of those whom they are leading.

If the energy in the future is not what they wanted it to be, leaders have only themselves to blame.

Today's top-down management wants highly energetic, conscientious people, but fails to see how it deprives these people of fulfillment of psychological needs that could stoke the energy.

It is difficult to show how a more systematic approach to getting the best out of people can come across as being natural and not mechanical or fake, but it can be done because it is a gradual attitude change. Once the attitude changes, the encouraging words are easier to find because people will be looking for ways to eliminate power-oriented words.

It is now more important than ever for the future of America for us to develop people who can recognize how the top-down approach to managing people has failed. It spawns distrust and causes morale problems in our institutions. Because of this, it will be important to develop people who have the skills and the courage to do something about the top-down approach.

The human spirit that America once capitalized on is being dissipated because leaders have neglected valuable research and refused to use it to develop good leaders. Far too many leaders are underdeveloped in terms of understanding human motivation. As a result of this neglect, good management is hard to find.

Autocratic attitudes are developed early in the nation's young people because our families and our schools are autocratic, and the attitude is transferred to our children. These attitudes are seldom changed as the young people grow older. As a result, they do not have the skills to create harmonious environments in which to live and work. They perpetuate the enemy within our borders.

Studies have proven that high levels of empathy, respect, and caring by a teacher can produce higher achievement in students and improve attendance as well as reduce the number of behaviorial problems. Yet, almost unknowingly, teachers avoid the communication expertise that would integrate these vital components into the learning process. Similar studies in business reveals similar results regarding motivation and productivity in the workplace. This will be touched upon in the next section.

Numerous human interaction errors are made daily in all institutions that have for sometime now begun to limit future energy. We are now able to measure these errors accurately and eliminate them. The attitude of top-down management is that the competition in the global market is so great that there is no time to be concerned with such flimflam.

How We Confuse External and Internal Motivation

Perhaps the most misunderstood element of the psychology of human development (which management of the future needs to understand thoroughly) is the difference between external and internal motivation. The lack of understanding of this one major concept is the factor behind the declining motivation of people in business, schools, and families.

We are confused about identifying things people in our society do that are intended to motivate, but demotivate instead. People such as Michael Jordan,

Joe Montana, Tiger Woods, Jack Nicklaus, and Walter Payton possess the zest and attitudes to perform to their fullest potential. All were *internally* motivated. None performed for the money or a trophy. The money, an external motivator, came *after* they were successfully internally motivated. Any company would like to have the work ethic of these great athletes on board. Great leaders in politics, medicine, education, and other professions all have well-developed traits of self-motivation.

The most critical part of human motivation for management of the future to understand is the detrimental effect that external motivational forces have on people as compared to internal forces. The plethora of evidence stacked against external motivation is conclusive, yet it is still the most popular means of motivation in business and industry, and in our schools and families. Why?

The ingredients for effective motivation are known, but because of our traditional beliefs in the use of outside stimulus—power, fear, coercion, expendability, embarrassment, and so on—there is tremendous difficulty in implementing the proper form of motivation in any institution. Such neglect is costing us dearly.

Dr. William Cook Jr., in his book titled *Build a Better You Starting Now*, discussed the nature of motivation:

> Millions of dollars and millions of hours are spent each year by businesses and by aggressive individuals in an effort either to discover the secrets of motivation or to translate these secrets into personal achievement or success. Those who seek to understand the "mysteries" of motivation or to achieve for themselves some degree of motivation are to be congratulated—first, because the seeking itself indicates a positive, self-responsible view of life, and, secondly, because motivation is indeed the beginning point of achievement.[12]

Dr. Cook goes on to say, "So great is the demand for motivational materials and programs that recently a veritable motivation industry has sprung up. Offerings include a variety of books, cassettes, films, and seminars that feature a variety of approaches to motivation, ranging from the sublime to the ridiculous."[12]

Dr. Cook explained,

> It is not my purpose here to pass judgment on any of these programs or approaches, however, I would point out that, in most instances, these attempts at motivation provide at best only temporary motivation. The "high" is usually followed by a sustained "low" until another infusion of

motivation can be found somewhere. Some say that this is the nature of motivation—"roller coaster"—but I believe true motivation is more permanent, longer lasting—in fact, unstoppable.[12]

Of course, true motivation comes from within; it is not temporary. Like the need for food, it is constant. Attempting to identify the universal lack of understanding motivational principles, Dr. Cook stated:

> The basic problem is that most people, including some motivators, don't really understand the nature of motivation.[12]

Dr. Cook added, "Human personalities have common characteristics so the general nature of motivation is always the same."[12] Of course, these common characteristics are the principles that Adler and Maslow tried to teach us long ago. Common characteristics are found in good motivational techniques, and they should be explored, refined, and systematically implemented in institutions wanting to move ahead in the twenty-first century.

Dr. Jim Tunney, a former National Football League official said in a motivational speech:

> Winners don't have a good attitude because they win; they win because they have a good attitude.[13]

Top managers of the future will have to know better than they do now how to nurture a "good" attitude.

Dr. Cook and Dr. Tunney give credence to the idea that we can do better in getting the best out of each other. We might translate these ideas about motivation into learning how to eliminate the spirit-killing language, how to be more empathetic and encouraging, how to rearrange the words to promote internal motivation, and how to forget coercion, ridicule, embarrassment, fear, and humiliation. It is time to give validation not only to solid research, but also to some well-developed theories and opinions that have been proven over and over to get the best effort out of people.

External motivation is a little easier to identify than internal motivation. Building good internal motivation in employees is the result of a manager saying something like, "You can sure be proud of that report; it took a lot of work." Just to say to someone, "That was a good report; you must have worked hard on it," does not stoke the fires of pride as much as the statement that includes the feeling word *proud*. Using the word *proud* put the statement in more human terms.

An arrogant, but common type of motivational statement found in management today might be, "Your report was a good one, but we need them faster and more often." Internal motivation is the result of good influence having a lasting effect upon people that will motivate them to complete tasks and improve themselves.

The motivational dilemma is better understood by realizing there is also a difference between internal motivation and incentive. Motivation to do well, to achieve, to strive, is a common trait all people have, at least early on, within themselves. Our society destroys this trait quickly, usually with self-originated or trial-and-error motivational techniques that include incentives that are always forms of an outside stimulus.

When a manager says, "Anyone who sells a million dollars worth of life insurance policies can win a free two-week trip to Las Vegas," he or she is offering an incentive and an outside, external stimulus. Management would do better to do things that constantly *internally* motivate people.

External motivation, whether reward or punishment, is at best temporary, at worst fraudulent, always disillusioning.[14]

Anything which is temporary, fraudulent, and disillusioning is a spirit killer to the highest degree.

One of the major hurdles facing the United States is that businesses, schools, and families are relying on external motivation (outside the person) and/or incentives (artificial, temporary, short-term stimuli). This on-going, but erroneous system of motivation is in conflict with what the rapidly changing times are telling us to do. The climate in institutions in the twenty-first century will have to pull away from external motivation and become more intrinsically oriented because the people within them will demand such treatment. The rebellion will be devastating to business because workers will do things not yet heard of when their psychological, internal needs are not met.

Even the future work force that management now says will become temporary or even contracted out (and therefore are at the disposal of management) will need to be *internally* motivated. It is still a work force subject to proper forms of motivation. People who have been programmed to be demotivated by external means by top-down management elsewhere will not all of a sudden become highly motivated in their new positions. Part-time workers, lacking intrinsic motivation instilled in them, will still not be the highly motivated people that businesses say they need to survive. These workers will be paid with fool's gold.

An autocratic system of people developing through external forces worked better thirty to forty years ago. The independence factor people crave is something more people, especially young people, are aware of now. This awareness translates into monumental problems for business when management does not have the skills to make people feel somewhat independent and to make their work meaningful to them.

External motivation can weaken people because it deprives them of the opportunity to use their own strengths and minds—the internal stimulus that people know they have. That is not to say that people cannot benefit from a little external stimulus like praise. Good companies, good educators, and good parents have a feel for not only the proper amount of praise, but also for the proper amount of external motivation. Just as important is knowing how to reach the goal of making someone independent, self-reliant, and responsible. That goal cannot be met by using external means as a primary force.

Following is a rather common example of how motivation is misunderstood. A husband and wife visited with a counselor about their daughter who was quite overweight. They had taken her to psychologists and a psychiatrist, and some weight was taken off through various programs, but it was regained in a short time.

In talking with the parents, the counselor discovered that on one occasion the girl mentioned that she wanted a motorbike. The parents and the girl worked out an agreement whereby the girl agreed to lose fifty pounds; then the parents would buy her a motorbike. She lost the fifty pounds and received the bike. Soon after obtaining the bike, she rode it around town to all of the fast-food places and gained the weight back. The motivation was external and did not come from within the girl herself. After a lengthy discussion with the counselor, the parents understood better how to approach the problem and how to avoid external forms of motivation.

Devastating is the word that might best describe the use of external motivation in the business world. The book *In Search of Excellence* identified some of the things that successful or "best run" companies do compared to other companies. Although not explained well in the book, these successful companies must have a nice blend of external and internal motivational techniques. They are not filled with the need-depriving, spirit-killing forms of communication present in most of America's institutions.

We die with our music still in us.

Oliver Wendell Holmes

If the future of America is to be a high energy, thriving, productive one, Americans must be allowed to get their music out. The music will be heard the world over if we can only plug into some of these well-researched, but seldom used concepts in human development and motivation from which we can improve how we go about developing our people.

Now that we know that leaders must know how to instill intrinsic motivation in those they attempt to lead, we can begin looking at different ways this important goal is currently defeated. The misuse of power is one of the major hindrances to instilling internal motivation in human beings.

The Common Misuse of Power

Power is a term that almost defies definition. Some would say it is the ability to effect change. President John F. Kennedy used power to discourage Russian warships from reaching Cuba in the 1960s. This type of power is easily understood and recognizable. Dr. Tunney, one of the nation's best speakers on motivation, mentions that there is power in all relationships. For example, a baby in a crib has tremendous power, and parents who have stayed awake all night to meet the needs of a baby have no trouble agreeing with Dr. Tunney on that issue.

Dr. Tunney also mentions that people have personal power and positional power. In positional power, a mother or a general in the Army might say, "Do what I tell you to do or else." A head nurse uses her positional power when she says to a young nurse, "Get the patients to stop hanging around your office or I will be looking for a new nurse to take your place."

Effective personal power is less visible and more influential. It involves *gaining* cooperation instead of using the traditional methods such as fear, humiliation, threats, sarcasm, and ridicule to force cooperation. Good personal power is something a well-respected leader has and can use to influence others to do things through good communication that involves encouragement.

Few leaders are very adept at influencing others to get something done. They usually resort to power, which is quicker but less effective. Leaders with good personal power understand the necessity to eliminate discouragement. They understand the importance of social connectiveness and building people up instead of tearing them down.

Using power is a little different from using influence, although misguided leaders believe that power is influence. Influence can bring about the same changes as power, but the action taken is less visible. The changes will usually be more permanent, and the impact on people will not be felt as harshly as it is felt with the abuse of power.

Power can be defined as the possession of control or command over others; domination; authority not so invisible. It is not difficult to see and hear power taking place. The current adversarial, power-oriented, discouraging relationship between management and labor is a telescopic view of the attitudes affecting the nation's institutions. Those who use it say this adversarial relationship is essential to maintain a democracy; those who feel it see it as a destructive situation.

In corporate America today, there is a defiance to understand fully the effects of abusive power and the spirit killers it produces. The effects, the aftershock, continually bring about unwanted workplace tragedies in our society. America has enough problems heaped upon it from other countries now competing better in the global economy. It does not need to miscalculate the effects of ignoring the psychological and physiological needs of people. Miscalculation will spell trouble in the twenty-first century.

Often catered to by the government, management usually tries to outpower the work force; chaos results. The spirit killers, probably already deeply rooted, dig deeper and usually bring about change, but in an unwanted way. Unwanted change in an institution is usually coerced, and power is abused. Influence is abandoned, and psychological needs will be unmet.

Excellent research has been done regarding the use of power and its effects in the business world, but it has been neglected. Even before *In Search of Excellence* came out, Dr. Thomas Gordon published a book in 1977 entitled *L.E.T.—Leader Effectiveness Training*. His observations of leaders in the business world led him to conclude the following:[14]

> The actual exercise of power involves some action that causes others to behave in a certain way despite their opposition to it . . . it makes them do something they otherwise would not do. The term psychologists generally use for the means to deprive others is "punishment" because to be deprived of something we want very much is felt as punishing. "If you don't do what I want, then I will deprive you of something you need." The use of this source of power is coercive, for the recipient feels coerced into compliance with the leader's solution.[14]

Intriguing are Dr. Gordon's words, "deprive you of something you need." This deprivation of needs has become a psychological game in America's institutions simply because of the traditional approach to human development. Even with all the research studies available up to now, American management still clings to coercion to get things done because it works quicker and can be measured more easily. Even our government believes that to develop people in our institutions in this way is a benefit to the country. It is not. Coercion, another form of spirit killing, deprives workers of the fulfillment of their psychological needs, and thus robs them of receiving meaning from their work.

Psychological needs, destroyed by the use of power, cannot be seen as readily as physiological needs. Seeing a hungry homeless person forms a clearer picture of unmet needs (physiological) than seeing a terrifying, autocratic boss who leaves unmet the (psychological) needs of his employees. It is not well recognized that the common use of power by management creates problems of motivation and productivity instead of improving things in most institutions.

Both management and government policies, laws, and regulations rebuke contentment of employees. This will have to change in the near future since the neglected research mentioned here continues to show that worker-friendly companies survive and thrive longer than other companies.

In education circles, it is well accepted that there is a direct correlation between how young people behave and how they feel about themselves. Using power on workers will make those people "behave in certain ways despite their opposition to that behavior."

There is little difference in thinking, perhaps subconscious thinking, between a youngster who joins a gang and an individual who joins a union. Some kind of need has not been met, and it is usually a psychological, not a physiological need. The gang member needs social connectiveness, belongingness, recognition, gratification, self-esteem, and some meaning. The union member needs the same and is often deprived of it by the abuse of power.

Dr. Gordon's research tried to inform management that psychological needs are powerful forces, and people will try to have these needs met in ways which they have not totally thought out. Most employees do not want to join forces against an employer, but their psychological needs are often as important to them as money. Business management in America is now running so far behind the research available that it is telling employees that they must not let their psychological needs get in the way of productivity. Being tough, prepared, and flexible, overcoming feelings of disappointment, grief, anxiety, fear, and humiliation are all sacrifices management now asks employees to make for the good of the company.

People behaving in ways they oppose is hurting America in the workplace. Employees taking so-called sick days when they are not sick is an example of power causing people to do something despite their opposition to it. It is known that absenteeism is a major factor affecting America's productivity in business, industry, and schools. Management just does not believe the research that autocratic, power-laden atmospheres are a major source of absenteeism.

Abused power on the inside of an organization causes management to spend a great deal of time on making the organization look better on the outside than it really is on the inside. Often more power is used on those in the organization who might blow the whistle on management in terms of filing charges, lawsuits, or grievances to relieve the atmosphere of misused power.

We must realize that the top-down, power-laden approach to motivation is laying the groundwork for future disaster. Stress is credited for causing several shootings in the United States Post Office. The Postmaster General commented about management, "Our methods are too authoritarian." He suggested changes.

In what seemed to be a look into problems similar to those of the post office, Dr. Gordon, in 1977, tried to warn management,

> Perhaps it is inevitable that coercive power generates the very forces that eventually will combat it and bring about a more equitable balance of power.[14]

Some way, somehow in the twenty-first century, the power that management now holds will be balanced out by the people working in our institutions. More than likely it will happen in one of three ways or a combination thereof:

- Unions will resurge.
- Government will regulate business more.
- Business will see the need to become worker-friendly in order to be competitive with companies that treat people like assets.

The last one on the above list is not likely to happen.

Power is transmitted in many subtle ways. For example, the use of the word *I* to motivate people is often a subtle reminder of the inability of a leader to use power effectively. The continual use of *I* by managers leaves a connotation that whoever is overusing *I* really means to control the people being supervised by using power and authority. The use of *I* faces a subconscious resistance in today's society. Its overuse can, and does, turn people off. One can imagine how employees in one company might have felt when they reported a boss used *I* forty-three times in a one-hour department meeting. Another boss used *I* fourteen times in a two-minute telephone conversation. A memo passed around by the boss in one organization read:

I want you people to _____ . I must have your reports by _____ . I want this back in two weeks _____ . I talked with Mr. Schultz and I decided to _____ .

Over a period of time the use of *I* gives off the idea that employees are not part of the team. The goals of the organization are not a we-oriented project. The use of *I* often implies that employees are working to meet the needs of the boss. We know employees are working to meet their own needs first and then the needs of the company.

The following letter, which appeared in a book geared for those who manage schools, is typical of how management has been trained in today's America. It vividly demonstrates the power of *I* instead of expressing a team approach to solving problems.

Feb. 18, 19—

Dear Miss Carson:

I regret the need to correspond with you on what may seem to be items of less-than-major import. Nevertheless, seven (7) latenesses to work since February 1 are hardly trivial. Although we talked on November 4 of this year about the same issue, namely your habitual lateness, and while some improvements seemed to come about, this recent relapse demands your immediate attention and concern.

On February 7, 11, and 12 you were fifteen (15) minutes late on each day, missing your entire homeroom assignment each time. On February 14, 15, and 16 you were twenty (20) minutes late, so that you also missed the beginning of your first period classes.

I am sure you must realize that such chronic abdication of your professional responsibility cannot continue. You are directed to arrive at work at the prescribed time. Failure for you to do so will so necessitate a recommendation from me to the superintendent of schools for your dismissal.

Obviously, an occasional lateness for inescapable reasons cannot be avoided; we understand and appreciate that. On the other hand, your pattern is hardly indicative of sporadic, emergency situations.

If you wish to discuss your problem with me again or if you have questions, please let me know. I trust I can depend on this situation being corrected at once.

Principal
RF: am
cc: Supt of Schools
Personnel Records[15]

The letter to Miss Carson was suggested as a way to correct "unacceptable behavior" under the heading "delicate handling of reprimands and other negative correspondence." Cited as part of a reprimand was the need of the school principal, who is the leader in this case, "to be ultra-careful and sensitive to the potential feelings of the intended recipient." It might not be interpreted as "so delicate" and "sensitive to the potential feelings" by some people. Following is a revision designed to remove the power. It attempts to be "ultra-careful" in relating to "potential feelings."

February 18, 19—

Dear Miss Carson:

As you remember we had a discussion in the fall regarding our agreed-to policy for punctuality, responsibility, etc. Your performance from that time until the first of the year was one in which you could take pride, and we encourage you to continue to build such a good record.

Recently, however, it has been brought to my attention that you have been late several days in a short span of time. This has been discouraging to us, and we have become very concerned about you since we do not know what caused you to be late. In what way can we provide assistance to help you maintain your punctual, responsible pattern? We are open to suggestions as we value you as an employee and would like to help.

In the past, employees have encountered personal difficulties which affected their work, and we were able to work with the employee and resolve the problem. We find it unpleasant and counterproductive to ask for resignations or to terminate employees and are hopeful you enjoy working with us. Please let us know what we can do to help rectify this situation.

PRINCIPAL

This letter is more encouraging. Encouragement has a better chance of changing behavior than power, threats, fear, and intimidation.

The two examples show (1) the abuse of power, and (2) how power can be toned down to promote a more worker-friendly approach to problem solving. Notice that *I* is totally eliminated in the second letter. The words are even arranged differently so the boss might come across as a more caring person, one who is genuine in his approach to helping someone. Correspondence such as this will need to be implemented in those institutions wanting to be more efficient in the future.

The "we" approach conveys the concept of independence and gives the employee time and assistance to overcome the problem. The great psychologists advocate the importance of self-governing, freedom, and seeking meaning in life. This is not to say that direction, confrontation, and input from those more experienced is not necessary. Confrontation in one's life is necessary for growth.

A boss who wants to defuse power and forget the *I* word can say, "Can we get all of the reports in by Tuesday?" To say, "I want all of the reports in by Tuesday," is different. It is more demanding and less personal. Gaining cooperation is different from whipping people into shape.

Conversations designed to change behavior must help an individual look inwardly at his behavior and see a need to change.

Successful psychologists and psychiatrists are skillful in using words that assist an individual to look inward and recognize self-destructive behavior. Those who want to lead effectively in the future need to talk with people in a somewhat similar fashion.

Keep in mind, people behave in certain ways despite their opposition to that particular behavior. A demanding boss can cause this unwanted behavior so that, in this instance, a report or two just might not be in on time due to the demanding nature of the request.

Confronting Can Be Risky Business

An unexamined life is not worth living.

Socrates

Confrontation, which happens often in a competitive society, openly opposes the views or behavior of another person. In a confrontation, there is conflict

present and power being used. The degree, the intensity, and even the dura-
tion of the conflict depend on the ability of the people involved to negotiate
an agreement. Some conflicts never end and, since most happen where people spend most of their time—at work, school or at home—valuable productivity time is lost.

Confrontation is complex, not well-researched, and, therefore, not well
understood. A confrontation usually comes across as a put-down and as an
attempt to punish or point out negatives about a person. Most confrontations
seem to be designed to help the confronter get a load off his chest rather than
to help an individual live or perform more effectively. Confrontations should
not be used often, but are popular in American management.

Effective confronting should be done in such a way that the individual being confronted understands himself better and learns something
important. If respect on both sides has been previously established, the
confronter can often maintain that respect, but only if confronting is not
abused.

One of the best ways of confronting is to respond based on the facts
revealed by the person being confronted. If the person said something or be-
haved in a way that merited confrontation, then the individual cannot deny
it. In confronting, managers can, with much practice, inform people of the
errors being made in a way that the person being confronted will willingly
make changes that will help the company.

Self-motivation is the only true kind of motivation human beings have.
Confronting with respect for the other person and being sensitive to his potential feelings is of paramount importance in creating an environment in institutions that is encouraging rather than spirit diminishing. Improper
confronting restricts the opportunity to create an atmosphere that will sustain
self-motivation. A respect-filled, encouraging atmosphere will unleash self-
motivation. It is only natural that if mutual respect exists, it builds up trust
and creates independence. A high degree of motivation emerges from such
relationships.

The attacking kind of confrontation, such as the one with Miss Carson, does
not work in the long run. Trust and respect vanish quickly in such confrontations. People get their backs up. These vital ingredients of any relationship cannot thrive in confrontations that emerge from the autocratic, top-down style of
management.

Far too often managers of today see managing as different from developing
people, yet they are one and the same. Too many companies in America today
make light of building up trust and respecting the feelings of employees. They

shun the psychological aspects of getting people to do things and are unaware of the cost of this neglect to the company.

The fact is, if Miss Carson must be fired, it should be made very clear to her that she fired herself.

Bosses, teachers, coaches, managers, and parents can learn to help people explore and teach them to do away with those destructive behaviors that keep them from becoming all they can be. This is the essence of sound motivation, and confrontation is a small part of it.

Prevention of unwanted conflicts, misconduct, and questionable behavior is the best medicine for any organization. It has been shown repeatedly in research that if people are managed in a "we" type, worker-friendly, cooperative atmosphere, there is less chance for friction to develop. Workers will not have to spend so much of their valuable productivity time patching up wounded spirits that the autocratic system creates.

In any organization, groups of people working together must be realistic and understand that conflict will arise in a competitive society. It is to their advantage to better understand that confrontations can be helpful if certain things are present. Confrontation must take place in an established relationship, one with trust at the forefront.

A confronted individual will not examine his behavior if he does not trust the person confronting. Such confrontation would cause resentment and future problems.

Some of the nation's greatest coaches have often used confrontation to their advantage. The late Vince Lombardi won major championships and was said to be confrontational. Other nationally known coaches have used confrontational methods. Their methods were, and still are, being questioned, but some have been effective confronters.

However, when they were at their best, Coach Lombardi and the others attacked the behavior of players and not the person. Coaches who constantly confront their players soon lose their effectiveness. The efforts of their players decline as trust in the relationship goes wanting.

Experts in confronting do all they can to establish team cooperation and respect for each other in order to reach the goals of the team. They may not be polished psychologists, but these coaches know they have to establish trust *before* confronting someone. They know how to confront and still get the best out of people.

Years ago almost any form of confrontation was acceptable in the coaching ranks, but now coaches at all levels are being fired for improper confrontation methods. Constant verbal abuse of players is slowly beginning to be questioned as those who work in the competitive world of sports seek ways to gain an edge. Some players have rebelled enough that they have been instrumental in having coaches removed. Managers in the business world of the future will have to give great consideration to ridding themselves of similar tactics as global competition puts pressure on American productivity and, hence, American management.

To the general public, winning confrontational coaches seem like dictators who use people only for their own gain. They are aggressive, high-profile taskmasters who are rough on their players. Regardless of the aggressiveness, the history of these coaches is clear. They developed a way to first establish trust, then were able to confront people and motivate them. The men who played and finished careers under them have great respect for these coaches. Players under them became winners and, later, winners in life.

One Green Bay Packer story is often told in which one player said about Coach Lombardi, "When Mr. Lombardi told us to sit down, I didn't bother looking for a chair." This could be perceived as motivation by fear; but fearful players do not perform well, so chalk it up to respect.

Most successful coaches, managers, teachers, and parents share an ability to judge the personality and mental makeup of a person. They know who can take a lot of confronting and who cannot. These successful people are usually very complimentary as well as demanding.

Many coaches, noted for their tirades on the sidelines, are often not as masterful as Lombardi in establishing relationships behind the scenes. Most coaches cannot be successful in over using confrontation to motivate players to win. Neither can teachers, managers or parents. If trust is established, a confrontational style has a chance—especially in the emotional world of sports. Self-esteem is usually well established in top-caliber athletes. Their egos are not as fragile as someone who has not had much success or as an individual who has not had people in his life who have helped him build up his self-esteem.

Coach Lombardi and similar style coaches appeal to the self-motivation factor most people have if pushed a little bit. They wanted players to play to their highest potential every game as well as have self-respect and pride in anything they do. Precision in building trust is something these coaches had to the extent that resentment did not build up against them. When coaches at any level begin losing the effort of their players, it might be attributed to mistakes they make in motivation and quite possibly in confrontations with key players. The same holds true for managers who lose the effort of the people they supervise.

Joe Morgan, former National League Most Valuable Player who is in the Baseball Hall of Fame, once paid his manager, Frank Robinson, a tribute that fits in well when discussing proper confrontation styles:

Frank is the kind of manager who can step on your shoes without messing up your shine.[16]

Trust, then, can be built and held onto so resentment and distrust do not bring down an organization. Refined methods of motivation, including confrontation, can be implemented into any organization much better than is currently being done in America. This will become even more essential in the twenty-first century.

Poor confrontational skills sap the spirit of people. They are a major source of America's managerial problems. Those who can honestly see good results from those they confront can figure they have a good feel for this potential spirit killer and can work around this traditionally lethal aspect of managing.

In tomorrow's America there will be a need to build into institutions the motivational skills that bring out the natural spirit people have to achieve and let it flow like water over Niagara Falls. This spirit is quite a force. Lombardi and other tough coaches knew how to get the spirit to flow to greater heights than many of their players ever thought possible. They have Super Bowl, Olympic, NCAA, World Series, and other championships to show for their skills. More important than the championships, they were able to get the best out of people and instill pride and determination in them. Companies in the year 2000 and beyond that have managers who do not have the skills to instill pride and determination in people are doomed to fail in a global economy.

How Listening and Responding Are Misunderstood

Intrinsic motivation cannot be attained in an organization unless a more encouraging language is implemented within the organization. The best way for management of the future to meet this goal would be to provide training in listening and responding. In order to eliminate the spirit-killing forces in any institution, it must be understood that good listening, not traditional top-down listening, is essential for people to understand one another. Good listening is the beginning of understanding, and good responding is the end result.

Most leaders, and for that matter, most people will say, "I'm a good listener." Current human development research studies do not reveal such a kindness in American people. Herein lies the problem. *Since listening precedes understanding,* managers must be trained to listen for subtle clues that can give them help in determining whether or not psychological needs are being met on the job. Often, American management misses hidden hints from employees that reveal they do not feel recognized, gratified, or even proud of their work. Responding to these underrated psychological needs is a skill sadly missing in today's management.

Many American people, some of whom are leaders, have an ingrained, traditional style of communication that deprives people of a sense of pride, well being, belongingness, and recognition. These basic needs are essential to individuals in any group if the group is to function at a high level. It does not matter if the group is a small family or a corporation as big as General Motors.

The question for management wanting to instill intrinsic motivation is how to fill these needs and eliminate the discouragement that costs productivity time. In each group, it must begin with much improved listening. Responding is probably just as important an ingredient to refine as listening is. Poor responding is the way the spirit killers being mentioned here are transmitted.

Listening for and responding to feelings is anathema to modern American management. It seems employees cannot prove their worth if they let feelings get in the way. Management no longer, if it ever did, takes any responsibility for morale. Employees are relayed the message that they, not management, are in charge of their morale. Management attitudes of this type are dehumanizing the workplace even more than is robot technology. As we will see, resentment increases and productivity does not under such management practices. The process is part of the unseen enemy that management refuses to recognize as we enter the twenty-first century.

Yet, responding to feelings and ideas is crucial for management. When feelings are not picked up on, management comes across as non-caring. Part of this dilemma is the fact that people can listen faster than they can talk. As people listen, they think about things other than the content of the words spoken to them. This secondary thinking has an effect on listening and contributes to poor responding. It gets in the way of responding to the real feelings another person is expressing. When real feelings are not responded to, they become minimized. People begin to draw away from each other if this happens.

This concept, understood by human development experts, is not given much attention by management, even when they do realize the working climate is one that needs improvement.

Information can be processed rapidly through the world's greatest computer, the human brain, but this rapid processing of information has far more effect on us as a culture than we currently recognize. The processing gets in the way of hearing exactly what the other person is saying. It gets in the way of picking up feelings that are not often given out in exact words. The lack of the ability of managers to pick up feelings has great implications for life in the future in America's businesses, schools, and families—its major institutions.

A person being spoken to often has thoughts that have little to do with what is being said. When people speak to us, we are often thinking about something else. This gets the listener off track as far as being able to respond to the feelings and ideas of the speaker. The constant inattention, not intended, subconsciously gives the impression of not caring about what the other person is saying. If the person is expressing some feeling, that feeling comes across as being ignored; this can be devastating. It does not make any difference whether the person is talking about himself or herself, the institution, or someone else; the inadvertent ignoring of feelings can have long range complications for productivity.

It is important to understand that thoughts and feelings are not the same, and that feelings are always right. People *think* they would like to go to a movie. They do not have a specific feeling for going to a movie. They do not *feel* like going to a movie. People cannot have any specific feeling for going to a movie. It is a thought process, not a feeling process. People *think* it is going to be nice tomorrow; they cannot *feel* it is going to be nice tomorrow. It is erroneous, in a technical and scientific sense, to say, "I feel as if I would like to ride my bike."

People do feel anxious, elated, discouraged, sad, or glad about events, but they cannot experience an event before it arrives. People can feel happy because they are riding a new bike, but there is no feeling connected with "I feel as if I would like to ride my bike." Those in management can, in their communication patterns, become much more adept at distinguishing between thought and feelings. This is important in terms of motivating each other. Understanding this difference, although complicated for some, helps in identifying feelings and, in the long term, needs.

The traditional top-down style of listening and responding is devastating institutions because to deny feelings being expressed is to deny psychological needs that research has deemed important to growth and development of the human personality. The over-reliance on analysis from the ivory towers is a form of poor listening and responding. Correcting this will be crucial to management of the future. The thoughts, feelings, and ideas of employees are seldom recognized. Over time, this avoidance of psychological needs deals a deathblow to management in any organization.

Since people act out behaviors, seek meaning, and pursue their inherited will toward growth based on how they feel and how they think, it is understandable why listening intently for feelings and ideas is so important in human development, motivation, and management.

Since people do listen faster than they can talk, some psychologists contend that most people spend 80 or 90 percent of the time they are listening thinking about themselves. If people are thinking about themselves this much, they have less time to formulate a good response to the feelings, ideas, and needs of others. In the following example, it is shown how a person might be thinking about himself instead of responding to the needs of another person.

A real estate agent for the Hardsell Real Estate Company is trying to sell a house (be productive). The agent has taken a married couple through an expensive home that has a two-car garage, three bedrooms, and a bath upstairs, and a bath and bedroom downstairs. The downstairs has a kitchen and a family room. The wife states to the real estate agent, "We like this house very much, but my father, who has arthritis real bad, is finding it difficult to get around. He is going to live with us. I don't think he can combat the stairs."

The usual response in this example is something similar to, "Maybe your father could stay downstairs since there is a bedroom and bath there." There is another response that is directed more to the feelings and psychological needs of the client. "Then the concerns you have for your father are of primary importance to you in selecting a home" is a response that empathizes and begins to build trust between this agent and client. A feeling of concern was picked up, responded to, and is promoting a good relationship.

Good listening promotes good responses, but poor listening cannot aid in responding to the basic needs of others. In the first response, "He could use the bath and bedroom downstairs," the feeling of concern that the lady held for her father was not addressed.

In this case, the agent's response is somewhat condescending in that it does not get down to the client's feeling some anxiety for her father. Some real estate agents would think it is a good idea to remind the client about the bathroom and bedroom downstairs. The time the agent and the house hunting couple spend together would be better if the responses were designed to build a foundation of trust. The same holds true for management in our fast-paced institutions. Today's management would say that building trust like this is not necessary. Tomorrow's management will suffer if it does not build trust.

If people think about themselves about 90 percent of the time, then real estate agents may, in a similar case, be thinking about their sales commission. This causes the agents to crowd out any response that relates to the feelings being expressed by clients. Meeting our own needs is uppermost in our minds as we respond, but often, because of this traditional method of responding, we let relationships slip away.

In management, when such feelingless responses are made, they create a failure to build trust with employees and customers. Customers respond to being treated respectfully and with concern for their needs. Current American management overlooks the need to respond correctly when customers express hidden psychological needs. Karl Marx wrote about the distrust created in a capitalistic society in which the feelings and needs of others are overlooked.

Similarly, S. I. Hayakawa said,

> The meanings of words are not in the words, they are in us.

Hayakawa's comment could help us understand how to interpret the feelings and meanings *behind* the words and, by doing so, eliminate mistrust. To be effective, management will have to look behind the words and figure out what feeling is being expressed. People do not often say, for example, "I'm discouraged." They say, "This job is not what it used to be. I don't like coming to work everyday." The discouragement being expressed is hidden in the words.

If someone responds, "Many people don't even have a job," he misses relating to the discouragement the person is conveying.

Responding to the discouragement builds up trust between these two people. The meaning was not in the words, but inside the person expressing the discouragement. It is a more facilitative response in regard to keeping a relationship on solid ground. In any relationship, too many responses that do not respond to the feelings cause the relationship to break down. Top-down management is a perfect example of authoritarian management not listening to those at the bottom of the ladder. It causes resentment and creates distance that will ultimately cause problems for the organization.

Continuous failure of a manager or any leader to respond to feelings, whether knowingly or unknowingly, can implant the roots for the growth of distrust and adversely affect any goals of the leader or the goals of those working under the supervision of this leader.

Human development specialists have developed "feeling word" lists to help people increase their awareness of feelings. Dr. George Gazda is one of the experts, and he and colleagues developed a list of these words. (See

Appendix A for the complete list.) Even though the definition of each of these words is known, they are not often used by people to describe their feelings. The words are used even less in trying to identify and respond to the feelings of people with whom contact is made on a frequent basis.

If management *and* employees, teachers and students, and parents and young people could only learn to respond to feelings on a more consistent basis, American business, education, and family life would improve. Using feeling words and responding to feelings helps to eliminate our unseen spirit killers. As a result, productivity will increase in any organization. Management trained in these communication techniques will help keep America competitive in the twenty-first century.

Learn How to Respond to Feeling, Not the Event

As just emphasized, one of the most dangerous spirit killers flourishing in American organizations is the traditional way people respond to the feelings someone is expressing behind the words they speak. We do not mean to be doing that; we are doing it because of habit and tradition.

Perhaps the best way to learn to respond to feelings is to make sure we are responding to the feeling and not the event. The feeling word list mentioned above can help, but another way is to make certain we do not respond to events someone is telling about. Too much time is spent in responding to events instead of feelings.

The importance of responding to feelings has been well-documented in human development research. Relationships are held together and they progress on a more workable, congenial basis when feelings are picked up and responded to. Trust and respect are ever present, and harmony is more likely to evolve, which prevents hostility and disloyalty from creeping into the relationship.

Once this type spirit killer takes hold in an organization, it is difficult to regain the spirit, enthusiasm, and vitality that all organizations need to be successful. If there is one thing big business management wants from an employee today, it is a high level of energy. This energy can be and is being extinguished every day in the workplace. Following is just one small example of how a boss misses the feeling expressed by an employee.

An employee says to her manager after an important meeting about the company, "I just don't think any of the district managers were listening in that meeting. I know they weren't listening to me. It seems my ideas and other employees' ideas are never heard or used."

The boss responds, "Well, it was a long meeting. The next one is Friday. Maybe then they will hear you."

The boss, as often happens in the top-down approach to managing, responded to the event (the meeting) and neglected the strong feelings being expressed (see below) but hidden within the words spoken by the employee. In checking back to the feeling word list (Appendix A), some of the following feelings could have been picked up on and responded to by the boss:

abandoned	ignored	left out
alienated	neglected	rebuked
cast off	slighted	rejected
displeased	hurt	overlooked

Surprised? The boss missed the feeling even with all of these feeling words available. A better response might have been, "It isn't a good feeling to be neglected," or "It does seem as if you were being ignored." The response the boss made lacked feeling content. It does not seem important, but research tells us it is because feelings minimized over time equals problems later.

In today's competitive, fast-paced business world, feelings are minimized frequently, and it is costing businesses plenty in terms of future energy of employees. In fact, there are signs of the United States becoming a feelingless society, and big business running roughshod over the lives of people contributes greatly to that unwelcomed era in our history.

Crimes are committed with no remorse, child abuse is on the increase, and firings and demotions are used to retaliate against good, hardworking people. Violence in the workplace is common. Fraud and corruption are even tolerated until someone squeals to government; then even the agencies to whom the reports are filed are often corrupt for political reasons.

Americans, in their traditional way, spend too much communication time in creating feeling instead of responding to it. An example is included here in which feeling is created rather than responded to. A father, whose son was accidentally electrocuted by power lines while climbing a tree, called the power company to suggest relocating the power lines to protect other children and their families so they would not have to suffer.

As we will see, the image of the company involved could suffer greatly simply because a company representative did not make a response that related to feeling. He does not show much empathy; instead, he makes a rather caustic response.

After a brief opening discussion with the father, the power company representative said to the father, "What were the boys doing up in the tree, anyway?"

Is the management representative building trust and credibility for his company? Is he responding to the feeling the father was conveying to him? It does not make any difference what the boys were doing up in the tree.

The power company representative, with his caustic remark, created feelings of ill will. Many bosses create feelings of ill will in the workplace when they respond only to events and therefore assume an authoritarian attitude in their attempt to get the best out of people. There is a major difference between creating feeling and relating to it. Lack of understanding this concept is costly to American businesses and will be even more costly in the future.

Some studies show that thousands of responses similar to this one, void of feeling, are uttered each day in large organizations. When feelings are diminished or ignored, intentionally or not, credibility wanes, and problems begin to surface. This is the beginning of how faith in our institutions and the management/employee relationships within them breaks down. Responses that affect someone's spirit ever so slightly can diminish that spirit if that person is responded to in a similar fashion day after day. A spirit that is killed gradually is just as dead. An employee usually does not have his spirit killed in one easily recognizable event. On the other hand, the exchanges that do cause the spirit to die are invisible to poorly trained management.

Employees become disgruntled over time. The top-down approach takes time to disgruntle people because managers do not *intentionally* turn off their work force. Most proponents of top-down management believe they are guarding against such workplace tragedy. Organizations will be better served if managers of the future study how to prevent the top-down approach from gaining a foothold.

Managers must realize that their managing style is what the workers eventually say it is and not what the manager perceives it to be.

The power company representative as well as a father used in the next example are both participating in another spirit-killing concept known as *being beyond*. Managers, teachers, parents, and others in positions of leadership often put themselves *beyond* the situation and feelings someone is expressing to them.[17] They do this getting beyond by leaving out the feelings being expressed when they form a response.

The father in the following example is quickly putting himself beyond his son's current situation. The young boy returns home from an important baseball game and says to his father, "Dad, I got three hits and drove in the winning run. We won!" The father says, "That's great! You must be choking up on the bat as I told you to do." The father's response misses the feeling of pride and joy his son was sending him. The father is beyond rather than with his son.

A better response might be, "Wow, that's really something to be proud of. It was a key game too."

An example of a manager in the business world giving such a response might go something like this exchange. An employee says, "Did you know the board of directors gave the brochure made by our marketing team credit for increased sales in the last quarter?" The manager responds, "That's what you are here for; helping to increase sales is your job." Such a response is void of feeling and does not recognize work well done. Even workers do not always realize how such caustic, *feelingless* remarks begin the downward spiral of the relationships between management and labor. Such remarks create wear and tear on morale, which affects productivity, the lack of which is usually blamed on something else—like a lazy work force.

Today's management shuns the tools psychology gives us, and this avoidance of the study of human behavior is taking its toll on America.

This powerful concept of being *beyond* is explained in a psychology book, not a book on management. The world of psychology and management need to be meshed together if America is to make rapid progress in the twenty-first century.

When managers make spirit-killing remarks of any type, they are on their way to being beyond the feelings of employees; they are not with these people in understanding their situations and their feelings about those situations.

Any management team that perpetuates over-reliance on analysis from the top is participating in the concept of being beyond. Top-down management is constantly beyond the feelings as well as the thoughts of the employees. This is not unusual in the United States, where companies have to use valuable time to correct mistakes that could have been prevented if the company hierarchy had listened to employees in the first place. If management could only stay *with* employees, the company would function at a higher level. A hierarchy that finds itself well *beyond* the feelings, thoughts, and ideas of the people within it will be in a constant struggle to keep pace with any competitor who is with its people.

Still another psychological concept that management seems to disdain is Sigmund Freud's catharsis, which means "to talk things out." If feelings are not brought out through the communication process, they are pent up inside someone. These minimized feelings are potentially explosive. The concept of management and employees talking things out gives importance to the need to refine listening and responding skills. Far too many companies, schools, and families have explosive situations arise that could have been avoided if feelings had been dealt with properly in terms of listening and responding.

There is a great deal of research available about listening and responding, but most of it is found in the world of counseling, therapy, psychology, and psychiatry. Counselors know about non-evaluative listening, or listening that is not *costly* to them in their relationship with those who seek their help. Management in America could benefit from training that would prevent costly responses, such as those in the examples just given. There is a *safe* way to listen and respond that does not affect future energy. Usually, the safe style of communication involves responding to feeling.

As with any change, there will be some discomfort in implementing a new, special language designed to improve listening and responding, but research is telling business it should be done. Authoritarian management denies the research because it does not see a need to or want to change. It would have to give up power and, as tradition goes in managing, it believes that would appear weak. Management of the future might have to decide whether to risk appearing weak as a trade for becoming more effective. Employees would not look upon management that responds to their feelings as weak, but as people who care about them.

In making an attempt to change listening and responding methods, it is best to start by reviewing the feeling word list and then trying to respond to the feeling someone gives us. A simple way to get right at the feeling is to begin a response with, "You feel as though . . ." or "It's like your feeling. . . ." To say to an employee, "You should feel proud that your marketing brochure increased sales in the last quarter," is to *acknowledge* the good feelings being expressed instead of disallowing them. Management in the twentieth century has not come close to recognizing the fact that it can do a great deal to motivate employees through good communication. The majority of managers in America have been brought up through the traditional, authoritarian ranks and have no idea what damage an insensitive response can do.

Managers of the future can give themselves a better chance to respond to feeling if they look at who is doing most of the talking in an exchange with an employee. If an individual is not allowed to express himself, how can feelings be expressed? Someone saying, "Gas went up again this week," is just making common conversation. Someone else might say, "This job is starting to get me down. They tell you everything to do. It is lock step. It's like we don't have minds of our own, and the union is useless." This, then, is a good opportunity for the listener to respond to feeling and offer understanding.

An old cliché that says, silence is golden, is often worthy to consider; but just as excessive talking is a hindrance to good communication, so is silence. Both sides benefit if people speak out and learn to develop good feeling responses. The spirit, energy, and enthusiasm that can draw people closer together and accomplish great things is enhanced with such *catharsis*. Silence must be used with discretion because it can never respond to feeling.

In trying to understand how to respond to feelings, those in supervisory roles or even best friends might want to consider that to say, "I know how you feel," is not a very accurate assumption. The idea that any person knows how someone else feels about a given situation can be challenged. It is erroneous to think that the feelings of others can be known because we have experienced similar circumstance.

Since it is nearly impossible to know how someone feels about a given event, it is important to try to relate to the often hidden feelings being subconsciously expressed about the event. Skillful listening and responding can help to avoid factors that might get in the way of good relating. These factors are our own values, prejudices, frames of reference, assumptions, opinions, judgments, attitudes, and analyses. These factors can, without our awareness, quickly distort that which a person is saying to us in terms of their feeling. Keeping this possibility of distortment in mind helps people stay on the task of relating to others feelings correctly and not reverting back to old methods that involve their feelings.

Even though there is no such thing as a perfect responder or perfect listener, this fact should not be used as an excuse not to make an effort to improve relationships. An effort should be made by people, especially those in management positions in a hierarchy, to become adept at identifying the spirit-killing forms of listening and responding so common to daily communications within America's organizations. Failure to improve listening and responding in the future will be devastating to American businesses, and the research tells us so.

Encouragement Is the Most Essential Ingredient in All Relationships

A simple way to describe that which research is telling management it should do to make people more productive is for it to be more encouraging. All of the spirit killers mentioned here are discouraging.

- External motivation leaves people dependent on others.
- Abuse of power takes the spirit out of people.
- Misused methods of confronting people thwart their enthusiasm.
- Poor listening and responding minimizes feelings that usually become explosive.

It should be easy for us to see that all of this going on in any organization will make it less effective.

To change the environment in our institutions, we must emphasize how to make people more encouraging to each other. To accomplish this great task, it would be advantageous to consider in more depth Adler's psychological theory that man is a social being.

Adler believed that encouraged people seek meaning in their lives and strive to take advantage of inherent talents. The United States has within it millions of people whose talents are not being utilized. Remember, Oliver Wendell Holmes said, "We die with our music still in us." Many of these people have been discouraged by the autocratic, top-down system of management they have worked under. They are no longer seeking the meaning to their lives that they once aspired to find. The top-down approach has taken its toll on them in terms of energy, enthusiasm, inspiration and vitality. They have developed apathetic attitudes towards life.

America is filled with discouraged people, and we know that discouragement is our greatest source of all kinds of misconduct. These millions of people are not sure they want to go up against a system of management that they see as being detrimental to the country and that is supported by policies handed down by those in ivory towers in the federal and state governments.

Millions of discouraged people have lost dignity, self-esteem, and self-worth, and are no longer interested in working hard to meet these vital needs. They want to avoid the almost absolute tyranny that caused them to be beaten down before. These people often find themselves uneducated, homeless, sick, or working at jobs far below their talent level. Large numbers of citizens who have, to a certain extent, survived the effects of America's top-down management system fail to vote and are afraid to speak out against the system. They believe they have little chance to change the system that victimized them. This behavior does not bode well for a country that needs to increase its productivity to remain competitive in the twenty-first century.

Our pathetic waste of human resources is perhaps our greatest enemy within, and yet the top-down policies bringing about this chaos are often lobbied for by big business and catered to by the government. As long as politicians are bought off by business lobbyists and make policies that line the pockets of CEOs, corporate boards, and their shareholders instead of policies that make the workplace free of spirit-killing management, America will not become all it can be.

Our entire outlook on how people are best managed, taught, and raised will have to change to bring about encouraging workplaces, schools, and families.

Adler taught "an encouraging view of man" that promoted things like fellow men giving each other self-worth, dignity, and a chance to succeed in a society where a cooperative spirit prevailed. If we accept the research done in *In Search of Excellence,* which told management, in essence, that a special, encouraging language is needed in the workplace, we see proof that Adler's views had soundness to them.

If current language in the workplace is discouraging, we should be able to break it down and find out what is so discouraging about it. Remember, psychologist Harry Stack Sullivan tried to show us that our traditional listening and responding habits play a big role in delivering discouragement. Discouragement is, as research tells us, passed around rather freely in conversations.

Ingrained, discouraging responses are brought about by years of passed-down, traditional communication patterns. They are meant to discipline, correct, mold, teach, and develop, and they become lifelong patterns of communication uttered every day. There is usually no awareness of the effect these responses have on others, either positive or negative. These responses are *unwittingly* taught to people by the significant people around them in their lives. We do not have to let the standards of today be the standards for the twenty-first century.

Following is a response that typifies the unsound methods of motivation found in most of America's institutions.

A first grade teacher, who is also a mother, is helping her sixth-grade daughter with an assignment. When the daughter experiences some difficulty with the assignment, the mother says, "Debbie, my first-graders can do that."

A manager might say to a young employee, "We have had people here for over twenty years who never made mistakes like that." How many more will stay for another twenty years?

It is obvious that these comments were made to motivate Debbie and the young worker. They are also put-downs, recognized or not. It is discouraging for a sixth-grader to be compared to a first-grader in almost anything. The well-meaning mother has had these responses ingrained into her by the culture in which she lives. She uses such responses without realizing the possible discouraging effect on her daughter.

The intent of the mother was to motivate; the effect was embarrassment. It is unfortunate that ridicule, embarrassment and humiliation are common, traditional tools of human development and motivation.

Here is another typical example. "You will never learn how to hit if you hold your hands like that on the bat." This is a disparaging remark a father of a Little League player made at a practice session. A more encouraging comment would have been, "You are trying hard. Try to hold your hands close together on the bat. This might give you a little more feel for the bat."

Beginning a response with "You will never" rules out any chance of change or progress. It can be discouraging because it conveys the idea that the young player is unable to improve. Far too often parents wonder why their children do not become interested in athletics or follow through once they show interest in something. The youngsters become discouraged. They do not want to do something at which they might fail because it is not the nature of man to want to fail. Too many spirit-killing remarks diminish spirit in young people, and they seek something safer to do.

Here is yet another example. A manager says to one of his mid-managers during an important meeting, "Cliff, it looks like you win the booby prize again for incomplete reports. How many times does this make now?" Comments like this are supposedly designed to motivate; but only serve to humiliate. Humiliation does not motivate; it demotivates and affects future enthusiasm.

Managers, teachers, and parents (really one and the same) constantly use these American-bred, lifelong patterns of communication that are adversely affecting productivity, learning, and human development. We should not find surprising the many articles and reports concerning a productivity lag and the declining condition of schools.

We ignore the teaching of interaction skills as well as the research that tells us how important it is to use psychology in human development. It is easier to stick with the traditional, old-fashioned way of motivation. The necessity to enlighten the country about the consequences of top-down management is a responsibility that must be assumed by nearly everyone. Dr. Lewis Losoncy, in his book *Turning People On: How To Be an Encouraging Person*, mentions that,

---

We live in a world in which we are all more able to discourage than encourage.[18]

People are more on the lookout for what is wrong with others than noticing what is right with people. Dr. Losoncy and another expert in encouragement, Dr. Don Dinkmeyer, believe that encouragement is the most essential ingredient in relationships. Together they wrote *The Encouragement Book*,[19] from which future managers could benefit. Too many managers in today's world look for books on the business shelf in a bookstore when the books they could benefit from the most are on the psychology shelf.

Discouragement and its partner demotivation occur not only in our words, but in our actions. Following is a common, everyday example that shows just how universal discouragement has become.

After receiving an invitation to play one of Chicago's well-known private golf courses, a gentleman was excited as his group teed off. Although a good golfer, he was not able to control his excitement. On the first few holes he did not play well, instead hitting his ball into a lake and a creek. As the group approached another water hole, the man noticed his caddy pulling several more balls out of his bag. The excited golfer, hoping to settle down, hit his first shot in the water and did not finish the front nine holes with a reasonable score. The caddy obviously determined that the man was unable to clear the water; this judgment was based on just a few minutes of knowing the man.

An encouraging remark from the caddy such as, "You can do it," could have been helpful. Yes, it is clear that we do not have an encouraging view of our fellow man. So many good things could happen if this trend could be reversed in our institutions.

Is this form of discouragement universal? Here is another common example. A basketball coach removed a junior high boy from a game and said to him, "You didn't even get your hand up to call for the ball." The boy hung his head so quickly that it looked as if the coach's words had the effect of a chain saw cutting his neck. The young boy went back in the game, but threw the ball away, then double dribbled and was taken out again.

A coach, who is a manager of sorts, with the proper training and understanding could have been more encouraging in tone. He could have said, "Jimmy, that was a good move to get open. The next time you're open like that, raise your hand and call for the ball. Help your teammates see you."

Instead of being reminded of his faults and mistakes (a maneuver typical of American management), the boy in this example is complimented about what he did well and instructed in an encouraging manner about how he can improve. People perform better after encouragement. Their future energy is still in reserve.

Suppose a boss says, "Didn't we talk about this problem before? You just keep doing it wrong. It must be done right, or I will have to get someone else to do it." This is a discouraging approach to get someone to do something. It is blaming, scolding, ridiculing, demanding, and criticizing. A more *togetherness* approach or a *socially connected* approach would include something similar to, "This has been a difficult problem to solve. Let me see if you have it down now, and if not I will try to help."

Losoncy and Dinkmeyer state,

One wonders why the positive effects of encouragement have been so ignored in the past. The major reason, we believe, is that encouragement challenges a tradition that emphasized the use of power, competition, intimidation, and autocracy as a means to human relationships.[19]

If any four words describe what is going on in the business world in America today, they are power, competition, intimidation, and autocracy. Now we can see why the research that would move psychology into the business world has been ignored. The inclusion of psychological concepts would challenge business thinking to its core.

Losoncy and Dinkmeyer go on to say that encouragers are people who listen and respond without judging or condemning. On the other hand, discouragers are described as people who are ineffective listeners. Following are a few other characteristics Losoncy and Dinkmeyer use to compare discouragers and encouragers.

Discouragers	Encouragers
Ineffective listening	Effective listening
Focuses on negatives	Focuses on positives
Competing, comparing	Cooperative
Threatening	Accepting
Uses sarcasm, embarrassment	Uses humor, hope
Humiliates	Stimulates
Recognizes only well-done tasks	Recognizes effort and improvement
Disinterested in feelings	Interested in feelings
Bases worth on performance	Bases worth on just being [20]

Managers, teachers, and parents would increase their effectiveness if they could keep these characteristics in mind. It would help eliminate our spirit killers and stop the blame game so popular in today's competitive society.

People are not born lazy or uncooperative. They are, in the traditional and subtle American way, *engineered* into such an attitude. Businesses then try to *reengineer*, as it is popularly being called, to get more productivity out of people and more quality into products. Management does not yet understand that reengineering would not be necessary if it did not engineer into people attitudes that promote laziness and uncooperativeness. Such attitudes are a strike back at misinformed management. This debilitating process is no different from young people striking back at authoritarian parents in their cleverly designed ways.

One major factor in this debilitating process is that young people can run away from overbearing, authoritarian parents, or at least stay away from them; but most adults have to have a job to support themselves. The lackadaisical, defiant, uncooperative attitude engineered into employees by autocratic, top-down management cannot be shown around the workplace or they will be out the door. Management of today has so much control regarding not having to change its incompetence that it is not only discouraging to millions of Americans, it is frightening to them as well.

The Praise–Criticism Dilemma

Another spirit killer in motivating people is one we might call the praise–criticism dilemma. It is known that a steady diet of criticism is not going to get the best effort out of someone. On the other hand, praise is rarely looked at as being part of the spirit-killing forces that haunt organizations. It is. The boss who says, "That's great; keep up the good work," may be using this praise to substitute for picking up on feelings. As we have learned, this can cause problems. This is no different than a parent looking at a report card and saying, "This is great! Your grades are good. Keep up the good work." The problem with praise is people can get hooked on it.

Young people especially can become somewhat dependent on getting praise and, therefore, can become vulnerable without it. These young people later move into the work force and, since they are hooked on praise, they become discouraged when they do not get it. It becomes difficult for even the best bosses because they cannot give so much praise to one employee without creating negative feelings in other employees. For managers to develop the proper blend of praise and criticism is just as difficult as developing the proper mix of encouragement and confrontation.

A continual lavish dose of praise may make an employee feel less and less satisfied with his work. Managers in American institutions are simply not as adept at handling this problem in human development as they should be. Praise can have a crippling effect if overdone.

Parents and managers who, in hidden, subtle, and unobtrusive forms, tell youngsters and workers to "do things that make us proud of you" are making emotional cripples out of people. The praise in the phrase, "I'm so proud of you," is common, but it is better, in a developmental way, for people to hear, "You can be so proud of yourself." It is more important for someone to be proud of himself than it is for someone else to be proud of him.

We need to rethink praise as we use it in managing people. While praise is necessary to meet needs, it is important to recognize when praise turns into control through the wishes or desires of others. Again, balance is needed. Controlling with praise does not motivate. It stifles, and originality and creativity are often thwarted.

Criticism is a popular way for people to try to change the behavior of other people in our society. It is important to look at criticism as a form of power and control. Managers, teachers, and parents weaken themselves as well as the people around them when they overuse criticism. Finding fault in others turns people against one another. Saying to a child who has just spilled the milk on the kitchen floor, "It's OK. That's why we have tile floors in the kitchen because tile cleans up easier," sounds better than, "That's twice this week. Do we, even at your age, have to pour your milk for you?" Acceptance and patience is not a virtue traditionally taught in American institutions. Non-acceptance and impatience are tributaries to demotivation and discouragement.

To be less critical is to gain cooperation, garner respect, and create an opportunity to build up the all-important trust that people must continue to strive for in working with each other. Spirits are then kept at a high level.

Confidence and good morale are in abundance, and the good results that encouragement brings are more apt to take place if criticism can be kept to a minimum.

There is a proper way to arrange the words when criticism is needed so that it becomes meaningful and does not cause resentment. Leave out the blame and work in some encouraging language when there is need to be critical. To say, "There are some errors in this report, but you will be able to correct them," is better than saying, "This report is sloppy. Other people around here don't make such mistakes, and neither should you."

It is clear that the praise–criticism dilemma is part of the spirit-killing force, the smothering force that is affecting motivation in the American workplace, schools, and families. Criticism given in the wrong way and in large doses is discouraging. Similarly, the use of praise can, in a more subtle, invisible way, be destructive and get in the way of the human spirit. Praise is important. It provides recognition, a basic need; but it is not often looked upon as being even remotely destructive, and its overuse should be given more attention in organizations.

Using Questions Effectively

Still another spirit killer is the misuse of questions in an attempt to get the best out of people. The improper use of questions has a more far-reaching effect on human motivation than almost anyone would believe. When discussing questions, it is very important to keep in mind the basic human need to be independent because questions can, and do, create dependent people.

Since the primary goal of motivation is to unleash creativity and originality, personalities must be formulated that will accomplish these goals without someone else providing the stimulus. Questions often keep us from this desired outcome.

Questions have unpleasant effects on people in two ways. First, questioning is often used to gather information about someone so we can tell them what to do with their lives. People who are bombarded with questions, then told what to do, and then do it, are not relying on their own strengths to face the challenges life presents them. They are dependent people.

The second unpleasant residue of questions is almost the opposite of the first. We have in our society people who are always asking, "What should I do?" They ask different people many questions so they might get enough advice to make a decision. This makes them dependent on others. The inability to make decisions and to become independent of others is one of the first signs of mental illness. These people are not the strong, mentally healthy people we need to develop. Our need is to develop independent people who become creative. The Japanese showed creativity when they mass-produced quality automobiles and nearly took over Detroit without firing a shot.

Even trained psychologists, psychiatrists, counselors, and other helpers can fall into the questioning trap rather easily. If these trained people can fall into this trap, certainly managers, teachers, and parents can too. A major reason individuals stay in therapy for months or even years is because they become hooked on the therapist.

Consider that the goal of a psychologist or anyone attempting to help another is to talk with a person in such a way that the person becomes self-reliant in a reasonable length of time. Managers, parents, and teachers—in fact, all people—could benefit from perfecting questioning skills because it frees people to perform more worthwhile tasks, such as producing something or learning something.

In using questions, consider that they often show curiosity about a person instead of interest in a person. Curiosity is a destroyer of trust, and we know that trust is an important ingredient in any relationship. "How come you were late to work the last three days?" can be changed to a less curious, more caring, interested and respectful, "Colleagues and I noticed you were late a few times lately. What can we do to help you arrive on time?"

Many people will wonder how people learn about each other if they do not ask questions about each other. It is not an easy human development and motivational concept to grasp quickly. Of all of the motivational skills and concepts mentioned as possible inadvertent spirit killers, the appropriate use of questions may be the most difficult to master.

People can increase understanding of themselves if they can learn to, in effect, listen to what they have to say about themselves. This means that thoughts and feelings will have to be reflected back to them, and this is not usually done with questions. It might be better to respond to a person this way: "I hear you saying that you feel discouraged about your job," instead of using a question and saying, "Why are you so discouraged with your job?" "Why" asks someone to explain behavior and gets close to disapproving of their position or even sending a solution.

Most people do not want to have to explain their behavior or have a solution sent to them.

It is better for them to be able to respond so they get their feelings out (catharsis) rather than being asked to explain their behavior.

Questions are abused in almost any organization. An employee might say, "No matter what I do, my reports are always the last ones in." It is easy for the boss to fall into ineffective questioning here and say, "When do you usually start putting them together?"

A more facilitative response might be, "It is annoying to try so hard and not meet a goal." This response can help this employee to begin to look inside himself for the improvement he wants to make, whereas the question does not accomplish much. Such responses can begin to instill the all-important intrinsic motivation that research is saying is so important for people and organizations.

A boss seeking improvement in some area from an employee might say, "Why not just do it this way?" An open-ended question that leaves room for independence and insight might be, "In what way do you see yourself improving on this?" If the employee comes up with the solution, it builds confidence and self-esteem, and eliminates the power that bosses usually abuse.

People working in the nation's institutions will be suspicious of questions if they are not given reasons beforehand as to what the questions are all about. Suspicion creeps in very easily now and helps promote the distrust affecting productivity. The suspicion can arise through the use of inappropriately timed questions and questions that put people ill at ease. Questions should be looked upon as part of the spirit-killing syndrome in the American workplace, but the majority of managers believe that they should be able to ask anybody anything at anytime.

Other Spirit Killers for Managers to Avoid

This book is not intended to be an extensive manual for managers to improve motivational skills, but is merely intended to point out how business is avoiding research in human development. The small amount of information included here is only the tip of the iceberg when trying to acquaint those in management with ingredients that kill the spirit of people and decrease productivity.

The spirit killers highlighted in this chapter are the primary ones being disregarded in management circles today. Following are other concepts of motivation, human development, human relations, and communications that should be considered in the overall process of trying to get the best out of people.

Managers of the future will need to include skills from the world of counseling in their preparation. Skillful counselors know that analyzing, judging, or evaluating someone's behavior is risky because the counselor's conclusion may not be the same as that of the person with whom he or she is working. This can set up disagreements and confrontations, and the chance to change behavior through instilling introspection into the person is lost. Judging and analyzing behavior is serious business, and these aspects of human relations are forgotten in the often insulting top-down approach to managing.

Although another difficult concept to understand, the overuse of logic sets up managers to demotivate employees. Logic is "sound sense," but sound sense differs from person to person. A solution to a problem may look logical to a manager, but it may not be that easy for an employee to see. Choosing the words properly, a manager can often assist in problem solving by eliminating his logical solution and skillfully allowing the employee to find a solution. Of course, this helps eliminate many of our primary spirit killers.

Far too often the problem in strained relationships that cut into productivity centers around false assumptions each person has made about the other's behavior. Our values, prejudices, frames of reference, opinions, and past experiences cause difficulties in communication. We tend to relate using our life experiences instead of trying to first understand the experiences of another person.

Opinions, for example, will vary on the following questions. If Bob is a heavy drinker, how much does he drink? If Dr. Smith is middle-aged, how old is he? If a few people answer these questions, there will most likely be a wide range of disagreement. Our own opinions may not come close to fitting the reasoning and the behavior of someone else. Exercises like this are used in human relations classes just to show the divergence of opinion on simple subjects that many might think are not so complex. Such divergence is something to consider when trying to understand another person.

One last concept to be mentioned that the research is telling us must be included in any attempt to revitalize our institutions is *empathy*. In global terms, empathy might be defined as the process of eliminating the spirit killers. It is really the ability to understand another person and convey clearly to that person that he is being understood.

Empathy is needed in our institutions now more than ever before. It includes being respectful, genuine, and congruent, which provides inner security and the ability to confront without damaging the delicate balance in most relationships. Transferring this important skill to the complex, fast-paced atmosphere in most institutions will not be easy. The skill of being empathetic may be the most important one for managers as well as employees to learn.

Central to restructuring motivational techniques is the approach to forming the self-concepts of people. This formation is best begun at home, but now businesses and schools must help refine techniques to get the best out of people. Complacency and denial in using researched-based techniques to form good self-concepts will not improve America's chances of increasing productivity in the immediate future.

A more cooperative spirit is needed as institutions will need to seek ways to become more vibrant in the twenty-first century. People must be willing to change traditional attitudes that hinder progress. This change must start from the top and be fully accepted as it goes down the ladder in any organization. Management in the twenty-first century must learn to develop workers better. Future success in the global economy may go to the country that concentrates on changing outdated ideas of motivation and human development.

Identifying the spirit killers is an attempt to clarify those elements that will need to be eliminated so organizations can become more people oriented, more worker/management friendly. It is important that leaders in our institutions understand that research is telling us that our language, as it is used for motivation, has to change.

The absence of a more encouraging language is the number one reason people in American institutions are not being as productive as they could be.

By eliminating our spirit-killing language, we can establish the only kind of lasting motivation there is—self-motivation. Instilling intrinsic motivation can be accomplished by cultivating relationships.

3 Top-Down Management: How It Fails Business

Introduction

Hollywood, which often tells America about itself, produced movies with titles such as *Take This Job and Shove It, Network* and *9 to 5*. These films vividly described job dissatisfaction in America. They revealed that many people seemed displeased with the way they were being governed in American businesses. Hollywood, in essence, helped bring forth an indictment of the top-down, spirit-killing system of managing, but with little impact for change.

Although Hollywood tried to help American business take an honest look at itself, its efforts were just another unnoticed attempt to warn us that something might be drastically wrong with how we go about developing people in America's businesses.

Hollywood certainly did not have the distinction of being first to show that improvements in the insulting top-down style of management were sadly needed. Evidence began to surface as far back as 1927 when extensive research involving workers was conducted at the Western Electric Company's Hawthorne plant near Chicago. The results of this well-done psychological study have, like most of the research, largely been ignored by those responsible for organizational development in the United States.

The Hawthorne study revealed that physical changes in the workplace did not motivate employees as much as did the employees believing that a superior was sincerely interested in their development. Modification of the work hours, breaks, and other environmental adjustments did not have a lasting effect on improving worker performance and boosting morale and trust. The superior showing interest in the development of the worker was known as the "halo effect," but management quickly forgot about this study since the conclusion meant that top-down practices would have to cease.

The Western Electric study may have been the first bona fide attempt in America to reveal that the top-down approach to motivation, and thus productivity, is not very effective. Numerous studies and company-spawned ideas designed to learn how to get the best out of people have come and gone since 1927. Most met with a similar fate as that of the halo effect.

Psychological studies were not needed for some people to question how they were being governed because they had physiological needs that were not being met. The famous Depression hit America in 1929, and workers were not too militant in seeking to have their needs met during these difficult times. Needless deaths and injuries were suffered in the workplace, and workers were treated with little respect. So-called "sweatshops" sprang up in New York as immigrants were paid alarmingly low wages for long hours of work. But as America began to recover from the Depression era, workers began rebelling against autocratic management. In the early 1930s, John L. Lewis, a spirited labor leader, organized the mine and mill workers to fight management for their needs.

In 1941, the Japanese bombed Pearl Harbor, and the nation's factories were turned into war plants to turn back an enemy clearly after our resources and freedom. Not much was said about the top-down approach during these war years as most Americans were united in motivation to win the war. Soon after the war, people went back to work in the private and public sector.

It was not long until complaints were being heard from America's work force that their needs were not being met. One segment of labor fought again for unmet needs when Jimmy Hoffa organized the truckers in the 1960s. Some truck drivers were wearing burlap sacks around their feet to protect against frostbite because the company would not pay to install heaters in the trucks. Even issues such as this that threatened human life could not make business leaders realize they could get more productivity out of people by paying attention to their needs and concerns. The Western Electric study was not important to business leaders then, and the psychological needs of workers still go unmet in most workplaces today. We began to neglect the research on what constitutes good management as far back as 1927 and are still neglecting it as we head into the twenty-first century.

Wars in Korea and Vietnam in the middle of the twentieth century slowed complaints about the top-down approach to management, although the approach was still hurting the nation. It was hurting us in and out of business and industry. Women began to speak out about equal rights; several race riots took place as blacks, perhaps the most victimized by the top-down approach, were still being treated unfairly. College students took college administrations hostage to deliver the message that they did not like the top-down way they were being governed.

Even though America flourished in the 1960s and 1970s, it was futile for those who could see trouble brewing from the top-down approach to speak out about it. The ideas of these people were quickly cast aside just as were any ideas that did not originate from the top. Then some courageous, future-minded writers were able to get their ideas published about how the top-down, power-wielding, insulting approach was costing America.

As mentioned, Dr. Thomas Gordon published *L.E.T.—Leader Effectiveness Training* in 1977. He made it clear that the use of power, fear, embarrassment, expendability, humiliation, and other spirit killers would make it "inevitable that coercive power generates the very forces that eventually will combat it and bring about a more equitable balance of power."[20] This is what business is doing now. By neglecting research on how to become worker friendly, it is creating a culture within itself that will create forces that will drastically change management in the twenty-first century.

Surveys of attitudes in the workplace were done in the 1980s, and they showed that most workers wanted to do a good job. They valued their work and planned to work well into old age. However, these surveys often revealed that workers felt companies showed little loyalty to them for the work they were doing and, as a result, workers were doing less and did not have much pride in their work. To those on the outside of business, those who studied motivation of workers, this lackadaisical attitude was a sign of management demotivating workers by not meeting both physiological and psychological needs. Industrial psychologists and social observers knew that the research was being neglected just as it was in 1927, but could not get the message across to corporate America. To management, the decline in quality and quantity of products was a product of a lazy workforce that management had no part in developing.

It should have been obvious to management during these years that people, not management, control quality of products they produce. The more management can create a halo effect, the better the chance that quality and productivity will improve. The question should now become: if people like to work and want to work, why is America finding itself in such stiff competition battles with other countries when our resources and finances are greater? The answer is that the spirit killers described earlier have taken hold. A nationwide program needs to be designed to rid ourselves of the traditional, top-down, need-diminishing style of management.

In the early 1980s, Tom Peters and Robert Waterman warned that companies could not be very effective if they did not have a special language that helped to create workers who had intrinsic motivation. Social observer John Naisbitt pointed out that people like to have input into those things that have impact upon them. He was critical of top-down management when he wrote:

> Traditional American management has adopted an insulting top-down approach to a worker's knowledge in his or her job. Managers in the United States have consistently denied workers the opportunity to make substantive decisions about how their jobs should be done. Only now are we beginning to see that this elitist strategy has cost America top honors in world productivity growth.[21]

In fact, it does not look as though management is beginning to see how the elitist strategy of top-down management is costing America. The fact of the matter is, when it comes to implementing a new management design, only lip service has been given to every study, book, survey, or report that reveals that something has killed the spirit of many Americans.

American management was informed in 1927, in 1977, and in the early 1980s by excellent sources regarding what direction it should take. Even in the early 1990s, an article appeared in *Time* magazine titled "Are America's Corporate Giants a Dying Breed?" Author John Greenwald wrote that GM, IBM, Sears, and American Express were "experiencing hardening of the arteries." He added:

Giants begin to falter when their managers, swollen with arrogance and complacency, allow themselves to lose touch with their customers.[22]

Since becoming acquainted with our spirit killers, we know that company management first loses touch with its employees and *then* its customers. Customers want quality in products and service, and employees control these ingredients. Therefore, management must look at the total make up of an organization if they are losing customers. It is a common practice of top-down management to blame workers instead of management practices that demotivate workers and lead to poor quality and lackluster service.

Signs in the early 1900s urged some of the world's largest employers, such as General Motors, to set aside the top-down style of management that had caused many huge companies headaches over the years. Top managers could not bring themselves to thinking that having employees share in company decisions would promote trust and a collegial, dignified atmosphere. GM was in turmoil for years and eventually laid off 40,000 employees.

Note that *collegial* is defined, "marked by power or authority vested equally in a number of colleagues; characterized by equal sharing of authority." This definition should remind us of research that gave us the halo effect, studies suggesting the abuse of power in top-down management, and the special language that brings about internal motivation.

Rebuking all of these ideas that proclaimed top-down management was at the root of America's productivity problems. Top-down management is now facing a competitive global economy with a force of workers not as enthusiastic about the way they are being governed as they once were.

Can the change to a more collegial, worker-friendly, bottom-up form of management be made? The past negligence of research suggests it is doubtful, but it is not impossible. It will cause pain and discomfort for those at the top of the heap as well as for politicians who have unwittingly supported policies that perpetuated the top-down approach to developing our people.

It is doubtful, because lip service is one of the favorite ways the top-down approach remains in existence year after year despite the research studies that reveal it does not work well. When problems occur in a company, it is common for top-down management to come out with new buzzwords that disguise the fact that management will operate the same way it always has. Workers have tired of words or phrases like "quality circles," "shared decision making," "empowerment," "worker friendly," and so on. Decision-making reaches the plant floor or employee offices about as often as Haley's Comet is visible in the United States.

The attitude of big business toward what motivates workers finally took a turn for the worse in America's business world in the mid-1990s. Following is just one example of how the business world continues to show complete disdain for sound research and how it is dangerously moving in the opposite direction from management practices that could keep America competitive in the twenty-first century.

Dow Corning employees were given a handbook titled *New Work Habits for a Radically Changing World*. The booklet was distributed by Pritchett &

Associates, Inc., a Dallas-based firm specializing in organizational change. Clients include 3M, General Electric, IBM, Eastman Kodak, Chemical Bank, Texas Utilities, Southwest Airlines, Ernst & Young, John Hancock Insurance, American Airlines, Bell South, and many governmental organizations.

In an alarming display of insensitivity to the research regarding organizational change and what comprises sound management of people, the booklet told employees the following:

> Somehow, over the years, we've been led to believe that higher management is accountable for employee morale. Nobody even seems to question this notion anymore. If attitudes go sour, the boss gets the blame. If employees are mentally down and out, the company is expected to provide emotional handholding until its people are happy again.[23]

The handbook for employees added, "We've got to get past a lot of this nonsense, because nobody is well served by this line of reasoning."[23] In almost the same breath it told employees, "Saddling someone else with the job of keeping you contented and upbeat is a slick move."[23] Were we not told that contented cows give good milk and contented workers? . . . Oh, well.

> It is a sad day for America and its work force when management, with all of its power, believes that it no longer has an obligation to do things that motivate employees.

All the research is out the window and in the wind. The halo effect and the special language are now considered to be only slick moves to blame management for demotivation. The attitude described in the booklet makes power absolute in any organization subscribing to such management practices. It is the epitome of the short-term, get-to-the-bottom-line, profit-at-any-cost attitude of management today. It is doomed for failure sometime in the twenty-first century.

On top of the most blatant denial of research in management and organizational change, this elitist, top-down attitude rebukes Maslow's needs ladder.

It defies Adler's belief that social connectiveness is important to people in groups no matter what their undertaking is. The arrogant attitude of top management reveals a disdain for the community in which it is allowed to sustain itself by using the people within that community.

The attitude about "getting past this nonsense" that management needs to motivate employees is rather evident today. Downsizing, reengineering, and restructuring have been the buzzwords in the late 1990s. All were slick moves that covered up discrimination, the right-to-work laws, and retaliation against employees who spoke up or acted out because needs were not being met.

Many American workers might find the following to be slick moves:

- Workers earning the minimum wage yearly are below the national poverty level.
- Medical care is often looked upon as a needless cost.
- Pension funds have been eliminated or robbed by some companies.
- Temporary workers are common and often receive no benefits.
- Contracting out work that could be done by company employees is a sign of the times.
- Employees are being told by employers not to look upon employment with them as permanent.

America has never felt such tension, and its effects are becoming widespread. Adding fuel to this tension is the attitude conveyed by management that "emotional hand-holding" is not something they are going to participate in. The very thought that management has any input into the contentment of workers is now a thing of the past.

Management blames all of this insensitivity on world forces they cannot control. They cut staff, and the price of stock goes up on Wall Street. All that matters are the top CEOs who get large bonuses after the cuts, the shareholders who benefit by selling shares they bought at a lower price, and the high-salaried board of directors who claim the company is profitable. Top-down management does not see all this as slick moves that demotivate employees. It does not see it as taking an emotional toll of people in a community who work for the company and expect something back for their community.

It is obvious, except to those at the top in business and most government positions, that American business is learning the hard way that its traditional, ingrained methods of developing people by use of power, fear, and expendability is a form of denial. The denial is no different from an alcoholic who swears he does not have a problem, that his behavior does not affect his family or other people. It is not any different from a parent who never relates to feelings, who yells and screams and uses external motivation, and then wonders why children are not motivated to become self-reliant and study and work hard.

Somehow management has come to believe that motivation of people in the business world is different from motivating people in schools or families. It is not and never will be. Remember, Dr. Cook told us that good motivation is the same for everybody everywhere; it is universal.

The change from a top-down approach to a more collegial approach, as the research suggests, cannot come about until attitudes of top managers, government officials, and top organizational change consulting firms and others influencing business acumen accept the research. Although the morale, motivation, and contentment of employees is looked upon as excess baggage for American management, it will have to change somewhere in the future. At that point, enough influential people will make their point that government will determine the conditions people live under instead of corporate America.

When the change occurs, companies will need to have those who understand how to develop a kinder, gentler atmosphere monitor everyone in the company until the atmosphere is pleasant to work in. We know this atmosphere can be created because some good companies already have it and are taking advantage of it. The problem is, the vast majority of companies do not have it. Certainly the opportunity is present for some worker-friendly, chief executive officer or a group of them to become the leader or leaders the nation is lacking throughout business and politics. They will have to recognize all of our spirit killers and help government develop programs to eliminate them.

It should be easier to provide gratification, meaning, and recognition instead of the stress, strife, and grief associated with most companies.

Companies make things difficult for themselves when management within them does not understand that the daily interaction between management and employees is the primary source of low productivity and quality. The daily interaction is the force that eventually leads to the data on surveys that tells us people are taking less pride in their work and are working less. As long as management does not see it has a stake in the morale of workers, productivity and quality will decline in the United States.

It is scary that we now know the flaws in our system of developing people, yet little is being done to correct the situation. It seems that government and business officials do not want to eliminate the over-reliance on the ivory-tower syndrome. The attitude is similar to a drug addict who wants to kick the habit, but cannot get the job done.

Top-down, destructive, abusive management is a habit no different from any other habit. Power is addictive.

During the transformation that is sure to come sometime in the twenty-first century, it should be understood that management has the right to check up on workers and see how things are going. In fact, workers, as the research tells us, want sincere, trustful, encouraging management who approaches them as being able and as people who want to believe management is vitally interested in their well-being.

The Attitude Dilemma in Business—Power or Influence?

For the first time in American history, the way we treat people, the way we go about getting the best out of people, is being questioned throughout the world. That is because we are wasting so much talent in plain view of everyone. Violence, homeless people, declining schools, lack of medical care, and our other social ills are a direct result of stagnant wages, meaningless jobs (or no jobs), corporate power, and a government bewildered by it all. Countries that are being given the chance to become democratic are balking because of what is going on in America.

The power corporate America has built up for itself allows it to hide behind escape mechanisms that keep the top-down approach alive and well. For example, company executives often blame the lack of motivation and productivity on elements and events outside the company. It is similar to education in America, where the school often blames the parents, and the parents blame the school for the lack of learning and development of our young people.

Failing businesses have blamed inflation, interest rates, the schools, unionization, and government regulations. Some companies blame computer foul-ups, shipping problems, the oil crisis, the weather, and other factors out of their control. Part of this failure dilemma is simply management's well-known ability to cop out and not take a realistic look at itself. Such a look could help business realize that failure and success are both products of human processes.

In pointing out the importance of *human processes,* Richard Pascale and Anthony Athos, both of whom are affiliated with graduate schools of business, offered the following:

> Today, world competition poses an organizational challenge that cannot be met simply by technology or financial resources. Technological innovations and resource allocations are outcomes of human processes. Our success is not inevitable. Our ability to compete rests in our ability to organize human beings in such a way as to generate opportunity and results rather than impasses, stagnation, bureaucracy and wasteful friction.[24]

For management to not take some responsibility for morale is to not recognize that almost every move it makes will influence employee behavior either for the good or the bad.

Current management in America knows that the fear of expendability is used as a motivational tool, and leaders cannot give it up because they are so afraid things will get worse—at least for them. Herein lies the dilemma. It is too risky to change because, for the entire history of our country, fear and power have helped us develop living standards unsurpassed in the world. It was explained earlier how freedom has become well advertised and how communication through the media has brought change to the United States. Because of this rapid change, those Americans who are astute observers of management/employee interactions insist that management must give up power and try more influencing, encouraging, humanistic, ways of managing.

Do It My Way or You're Fired, an enlightening book, revealed,

---

> There is growing agreement with Pehr Gyllenhammer, the veteran head of Volvo, that management can no longer be based on power. In most shows of power today, observes Gyllenhammer, the workers will "win" and management will "lose," though the inevitable result sooner or later is that everyone loses.[25] Ewing, David W., *Do It My Way or You're Fired,* John Wiley and Sons, Inc., New York, NY, © 1983, p. 11. Reprinted by permission of John Wiley & Sons, Inc.

The author of the book, David W. Ewing, also wrote for management to consider,

> *If there has been any lingering doubt about the importance of professional management, that doubt should now be erased forever. Employee dissidence makes the task of the manager not only more difficult and challenging than ever before, but also more indispensable.*[25]

By using the words "professional management," it must be assumed that Mr. Ewing was referring to management that could operate without using power. He indicates that well-trained, professional people in human development are needed because the employee dissidence caused by current management techniques is getting worse.

Power is a mind-set, as is the top-down style of management. Mind-sets are difficult to change. The longer they persist, the better chance they have of becoming securely anchored. Business management in the United States today, supported by misinformed organizational change firms and our bewildered government, is well on its way to making such power-oriented attitudes so entrenched in the American culture that the forces needed to change them could get ugly.

The abuse of power becomes almost like an obsession or compulsion. (An obsession is a thought that recurs often, and a compulsion is an act that must be repeated, like washing hands fifteen times a day.) These psychological terms can be accurately applied to today's managers. They are compelled or obsessed to use power because that is how they have been taught to deal with people. We need to become more informed as to how this power orientation becomes part of a person's personality and how it becomes almost all consuming to managers.

The most neglected resource in the United States is the intellect, inspiration, and dedication of the American people to make life better for themselves. When power is used on them, it stifles ambition, shatters dreams, and belittles dignity. Why, then, do we make laws, flaunt a tradition, and deny a past that favors an abuse of power that hinders development of the inborn traits common in every man? It is a dilemma that not only the American people suffer from, but the rest of the world as well.

Management must realize that workers in America currently spend a great deal of time just trying to balance out the abuse of power. Of course, this time could be better used as productivity time. Power was not so noticed in the past; things were different. As Ewing wrote, "In generations past, employees in textile mills, automotive factories, steel mills, and railroads sold their time and stamina. They were more or less interchangeable, like worker ants."[25]

Today's workers try to balance power when they discover they are not being paid a fair share of the profits that greedy corporate boards of directors, shareholders, and CEOs are taking in. They balance power by not producing as much or working as hard because the effort does not pay off for them.

In the modern workplace there are now "specialists" who, according to David Ewing, "have unique power over the organization. They can cripple it, if they want to. They can hijack it. They can paralyze it. Simply by withdrawing, they can devastate it."[25]

Management mistakenly interprets this dissident behavior as slackening or greed when it is usually an attempt to get an equitable return for efforts and psychological needs. Pay is often locked into a contract; effort is not. Effort must be nourished, cultivated, and inspired from within workers, but current management does not see the need to "cultivate relationships."

When people rebel against abusive authority and misinformed management, the use of power intensifies, and productivity suffers even more. The abuse of power has now reached an explosive stage as our working history has developed over the years. How many more days or years do we have before some of the world's developing countries blow past us in terms of production? How many countries in the world are now safer to live in than the United States? How much of this lack of safety and security can be attributed directly to governmental policies that perpetuate tension in people?

More people working on an independent basis, but with wholesome, congenial input from others around them, are very much needed in the workplace. More gratification and inner satisfaction comes from self-reliance, but American business does not understand how this independence can turn into better productivity. It does not understand how to fulfill the inner needs and tap the potential of people. As we approach the twenty-first century, management does not even think it is important to fulfill inner needs of employees or even to get training in an attempt to bring out potential.

In the book *In Search of Excellence,* which offered so much in terms of research, the authors noted that one leader pointed out to them the following:

Until we believe that the expert in any particular job is most often the person performing it, we shall forever limit the potential of that person, in terms of both his own contributions to the organization and his own personal development.[26]

We need more leaders who recognize such important psychological aspects of work. Being able to contribute to an organization gives one great pride, and companies can ride this pride a long way. More important, the personal development in terms of gratification and self-esteem a worker might obtain by making a contribution can help make this worker a loyal, hard-working teammate of top management. Good teams in the world of sports are often referred to as "having good chemistry." Management should use current research to figure out ways to create this chemistry and make their companies winners.

Many workers would fall over in their tracks if the boss said, "How do you think this should be done?" It would be hard to believe in most companies if the boss said, "We think you can solve this problem for the company. Can you come up with some answers for us?" Even more unbelievable would be management saying, "In what ways do you think we could improve this operation?"

Soliciting help like this shows weakness on the part of the leader under today's standards for management. Not being able to solve the problem himself and, heaven forbid, having to consult with someone whom he supervises, is just not the way American organizations are set up. There are times lip service is given, but rarely does it turn into anything in which a worker feels he has become an intricate, decision-making part of the organization. Decisions have to come down from the ivory towers or they probably are not going to be accepted. This selfish, elitist thinking defies employees to take part in the decisions of management, and research tells us this is hurting most companies.

Still another attitude dilemma involving power versus influence is one that encourages workers to *challenge* management. This idea is almost unheard of in the United States. Who, with the archaic, fire-at-will laws still solidly in place in most states, would dare challenge corporate decisions? It is still a "do it my way or hit the highway" form of management in the United States. This change, where challenges are welcomed, will be extremely difficult to implement. Few company executives are prepared to put up with what they see as guff, nonsense, and uneducated complaints of people whom they see as poorly prepared workers.

Open expression is a no-no in most businesses today. The lack of it is a sign of lack of trust. Open expression is best done by a large group of employees, but even then it is risky. An individual, who may just have a good idea, is usually so afraid of what top-down management can do to him that many good ideas that would improve companies go unheard. Freedom of speech is not given the protection in the United States that politicians would like to believe. Business management runs well ahead of the government in ways to get around the civil rights laws that have been on the books for years. Mass layoffs often include those workers who are speaking out or complaining of unfair treatment in the workplace. Often, people who speak out are older workers who know the business and know how to improve it, but business management of today sees these people as being a nuisance and gets rid of them in the wake of downsizing, restructuring, or reengineering.

Standardizing jobs in the workplace is simply another form of power. Standardizing makes it easier for management to see if someone is straying off course, doing things differently, or getting out of line. It chokes creativity and originality, but management insists it is easier to manage and is therefore more productive. This style has not promoted social connectiveness; it does not promote trust and does not meet needs of gratification and recognition.

Some workers, unfortunately, seem to enjoy the lockstep form of work that standardization brings because they do not have to think or be creative. There are too many workers in today's America who have been beaten down by the current system of management; they do not want to have to direct their thoughts to the improvement of a company that has put them down so often. These discouraged workers keep their creativity—their music—inside and enjoy standardized jobs so they can direct their thoughts to more personal matters.

Some managers seem to believe that standardizing jobs is the best way to deal with the cultural differences now found in the workplace. They do not understand that good motivation is not a cultural phenomena, but a human development fact of life for all races, creeds, and colors. Gratification is a need of all human beings in any culture, as is security. Most people would like to have the chance to build strong self-esteem.

Power diminishes the intimacy, the social connection, the togetherness that people need to make any institution work. Influencing people to get along with each other and share in the growth of a company will be more essential to management in the future as competition from other countries increases the pressure on American companies to do the right things to keep them vibrant. By neglecting research that tells us, in essence, that intimacy and social connectiveness are essential for *sustained* productivity, American management teams are cheating themselves and the people around them.

Lest we forget, President Roosevelt told us over fifty years ago that we should cultivate the *science* of human relationships. The first country to do so on a grand scale will move ahead in the global economy. The good companies in America, the nice places to work, are going along with this advice. They bend over backward to keep employees happy. They hire instead of fire, and show empathy by providing medical care and other benefits. It is sad for America that management teams in the majority of companies are beginning to reject the idea that they owe employees anything but a day's pay. These companies will backslide because they have foreclosed on the idea of cultivating human relationships and are a long way off from even thinking of such "nonsense" as being scientific.

Many companies have built up a power base within their management teams. They deal with employees in such a manner that they come across as being superior people while, to them, the employees are inferior persons hired to perform duties for the company. These dictatorial, autocratic attitudes alienate employees, and the ability of management to influence the work force to be productive is forever lost. This form of power is invisible to management, but costly.

If people sense that management has given up on them by using the authoritarian approach to motivation, this promotes disloyalty. Identifying the fact that loyalty is slipping away is a sure sign that management needs an overhaul. Power-oriented management usually practices denial even when it sees signs of some loyalty slipping away. Workers have to hide their disloyalty in this day and age. The American workforce has become skillful at hiding disloyalty from employers because it is not easy to find another job. This is exactly what abused power does—it forces feelings underground. Productivity is affected by disloyalty, but top-down management does not see where it had any input into the problem.

Too many managers believe that, because employees seem to relate well with them and say they like them, things are going well in terms of the employees being satisfied with work.

The atmosphere in most American companies is so riddled with fear of expendability that workers are afraid to tell a boss what they think about his methods of managing.

Managers of today are being taught to operate under the pretext that good jobs are so hard to find that feelings about work should not make much difference to them. How can it be productive when employees come to work each day trying to figure out how not to have to work under their present management any longer?

We should not dismiss the idea that tension on the job is a major cause of the increased violence in our society.

Using illegal drugs to escape from the stress-filled work environments is a full-blown cultural phenomenon of which the United States cannot be proud.

It may seem harsh to blame a significant portion of our drug culture on authoritarian management, but if people had better prospects of finding a job working for good management, they would not turn to the abuse of drugs and alcohol that often lead to violence.

The insecurity of the work force will cause it to become an even more powerful force behind political change in the twenty-first century.

It is unfortunate that the government officials who often replace those who have helped perpetuate the disenchantment of working America do not yet understand the deep-rooted disillusionment of the American work force. It is even more disturbing that the work force cannot explain in the needed terms that top-down authoritarian management takes away rights, dignity, and creativity. These people just know they do not feel good about how they are managed. The snail-paced attempt by management and our elected officials to make changes for the better is slowly killing American production.

Informed Americans know that most members of Congress are afraid to speak out against big business because it is the big companies that contribute large sums of money to keep them in their offices. The ever-increasing tense, violent environment in which we live is being nurtured by money from big business lobbyists and the power-oriented methods they are allowed to use to develop our people. This fraudulent practice will have to stop sometime in the twenty-first century. It will cease only when government and big business see that the power used on people regarding their jobs is creating the tension that leads to the violent, tension-filled environment.

Consider also that similar power-laden management practices are copied and used in our poorly managed schools so that tension builds up in young people working under autocratic administrations. We know that drug use is not slowing down in young people partly because of the way they are being governed. The demise of job security, health care and pensions, and good paying jobs does not give young Americans a pleasant vision of the future. The outlook for a safe and secure future seems far away for many young people, and many develop an apathetic attitude that can lead to drugs or non-productive life styles.

More and more, the basic need of security which Abraham Maslow deemed most important, is being denied. Predictably, this denial is causing tension in America that is being expressed by people in ugly, unsavory ways. It will continue until people become more secure.

America cannot continue to allow power rather than influence to be used to develop people and still remain competitive. It is essential that we examine long held beliefs about work and management and make constructive changes. Regarding change, Pascale and Athos wrote:

> A developing society requires departure, change and novelty in language, in concepts, and in the way of doing things. There has to be creative movement, at least at fairly frequent intervals. A society in a changing environment is doomed if it does not produce "managerial" innovations which break inherited molds of perception, old patterns of behavior, and prior expressions of beliefs and values.[24]

Looking back in our history we see that, since we neglect research, our institutions are managed roughly the same way as they were in the early 1900s. Power, coercion, fear, and expendability are probably now used more than ever before. We have not changed our novelty in language or in concepts, and not much in the way of doing things. Managerial innovations which break molds of perception and old patterns of behavior have been offered by informed sources in research, but cast aside by ivory tower managers.

If we are to be in control of our own destiny, which will be challenged in the twenty-first century, the above-mentioned departures from our normal ways of doing things must take place. As has been pointed out, changing our everyday language in the workplace is a key to the future; excellent research studies have told us so several times. A few good companies have made these managerial innovations, but the United States will need a lot more good companies to survive in the years ahead.

We need to look back, take stock of where we have been, where we are, and where we want to be, and consider that our technology and money have not changed the way we go about getting the best out of people. In fact, the technology, along with the top-down management style, is dehumanizing the workplace. Add to this the greed we now see revolving around the money, and we should be able to see that our society is not moving in an acceptable direction.

Politicians constantly talk about the shape in which we are going to leave our country for children in the future, for their grandchildren. There is real concern for the future, but no creative movement to change the way we develop our people. There is movement away from, rather than toward, the realization that our institutions are social in nature and that all people in them, from the top to the bottom, will have input into the success or failure of the organization. Our recent history tells us that a just few people make the deci- sions, and the rest of the troops become disenchanted because they do not get to take part. This elitist approach is in direct opposition to what good human development really is, and it is in opposition to the research.

Good leaders lead by picking up from those under their supervision what is needed to keep their motivation high. When most of the needs are not met, conflict will, by human nature, arise. The media reports on almost a daily basis about conflicts in the workplace between an employer and employee. Often these conflicts turn into shootings, hostage situations, or some other type of violence. The needless tension strains our country to its limits, and it is all because people are trying to work together to produce something or offer a service. The spirit killers are far more responsible for creating conflict than any of us would like to believe. We tell ourselves the words arranged the wrong way just cannot have that much effect on a nation, but they do.

Our businesses and even our schools have not changed much in the basic approach to getting the best out of people. Cosmetic changes have been made in institutions where a few knowledgeable people know that changes need to be made, but the top-down style of management cleverly holds the status quo. Influence could have been substituted for power, but did not quite make the breakthrough; and the institutions do what they can to protect their images on the outside as they suffer with the abuse of power on the inside.

Restructuring, reengineering, downsizing—whatever we want to call it— has been going on for sometime now, but it is not increasing productivity as so designed. Such actions are taken because businesses feel the pressures of the global economy and a need to get more out of fewer people. But by downsiz- ing, management is only creating a consistent demotivational element for workers.

Special Language and Special Actions Develop Winners

Research has all but begged us to change our attitude about human develop- ment and motivation. It is difficult for people in a culture to see how their traditional language affects motivation. The simple misplacement of words is, in part, responsible for the growing dissatisfaction with management in our institutions. Union and management disputes are prolonged by misuse of words. Recognition, belongingness, gratification, and self-esteem are en- hanced or hindered by words.

Alluded to earlier was the investigation by Peters and Waterman into what separates the good companies from the bad. They noted, "The language used in talking about people was different."[26] They found that in the good companies, the first significant factor in fostering intrinsic motivation was the language spoken in the company. The language, we must assume, was void of our spirit killers and especially void of power. It was more encouraging, influential, and respectful toward employees.

Following is an example of how the language used in a company can be influential instead of power-filled. The example could be looked upon as the beginning of a special language that influences rather than uses power to get things done.

Bill Hewlett of the well-managed Hewlett-Packard Company discovered an important lab stock door locked. It was to be kept open at all times. He left a note on the door for all employees that said, "Don't ever lock this door again. Thanks, Bill."[26] He scolded, used some power, but did thank employees. It is interesting to note that the words "don't ever" are threatening. It is more influential and encouraging to say, "We need to keep this door open at all times," or "This door must always be left open. Thanks, Bill." These words promote team play because of the word *we*, and have a little better flavor to them. They influence instead of direct.

The suggested wording to the small problem mentioned above is a little more pleasant and does not begin to diminish the spirit of employees. The "don't ever" example is a beginning, even though it is a small one, of spirit-killing words gently creeping into a well-run company. A continual pattern of threats, no matter how small, will wear down employees over time.

Perhaps the most important part of the research that management in America is avoiding is the implementation of a special language. Adding at least some credence to that notion is a statement by Fran Tarkenton, the record-setting quarterback of the Minnesota Vikings and New York Giants, now working to improve management practices. On managing people, he said,

---

I want to work in a positive environment. I don't want to work in a place surrounded by negatives where people are getting 'chewed out' and screamed at. All of the data is clear. When you shout at someone you may get an immediate reaction, but their productivity will drop in the long run.[27]

He continued, "We must learn how to talk with co-workers and people we supervise. What can we do to help them? Are we doing anything that hinders them in their jobs? How can we make our 'team' better?"[27] Tarkenton also noted,

---

It's really the responsibility of top management to create a positive environment. But some of the managers made it to the top because they were tougher and more aggressive than anyone else. Now they must adopt a new, more positive attitude toward the people who work for them. We've got to get the message across to managers that a positive environment has a positive effect on productivity.[27]

This view is in direct conflict with the view of management's role as described to Dow-Corning employees in the booklet titled *New Work Habits for a Radically Changing World*. Recall that the booklet informed employees that management is no longer responsible for employee morale, and "We've got to get past a lot of this nonsense." The research over the years supports Tarkenton's ideas rather than the idea in the booklet given to Dow-Corning employees.

Tarkenton agrees that, "It's really the responsibility of top management to create a positive environment." He alluded to what might be interpreted as a vote for the special language when he noted that, "Few people seem to know how to give negative 'feedback.' You must not embarrass people. Instead you've got to help them learn why they made a mistake and what they can do to correct it."[27]

He stated that he "always appreciated the coach who became a teacher and suggested how I could improve. But I learned nothing from a coach who insulted me. Except to dislike the coach."[27] Herein lies the problem with management in today's America.

Tarkenton made it clear that the way we use words and the way we go about killing spirits is something that must be changed in the way people are managed. In order for those in management to become consistently encouraging managers, they must learn to break down traditional words and phrases, and from this breakdown develop a special language that good companies already have.

The majority of managers in the United States today do not embrace a style that provides empathy to people. They have seen coaches scream and yell at players, then determined that this is the best way to get people to do things. Most have been brought up in homes that use fear and other spirit killers to motivate. These managers believe that to rearrange their words so they have a more pleasant ring to them is bad for people. Relating to feelings and using-*softer*, less power-oriented words would, according to these managers, soon make it impossible to get people to do anything. We can classify this rationalization as another cop-out to help maintain the top-down approach which seems to management of today to be so much easier to administer.

Motivation for productivity in business is not only stymied by autocratic language, but also by autocratic actions. Some attempts have been made in the research to examine the effect of the actions of managers on employees. Studies show that the desk of a top manager can serve as a barrier to the more intimate working climate research tells us we should strive to create. Managers who call people in for a conference, then sit behind their large desks do not create an atmosphere of social connectiveness, of intimacy, of togetherness. Desks arranged in open proximity deliver a message of closeness, and such an arrangement can diffuse power.

Bosses can be more effective by moving around and meeting with employees on what might be called a more common ground away from the power-laden boss's office. Keep in mind the halo effect, the idea based in research done in 1927 that management could be more effective if it gave the impression, by words and actions, that it cared about the well-being of employees. Remaining in the office and calling people in to give orders implies power and diminishes the idea that people are equal in dignity and self-worth. Using special language and special actions has an obvious sign of diplomacy and class to it, whereas authoritarian management lacks the class and dignity that respected leaders are able to project.

The commonly accepted traditional phrases of management such as, "I need to talk to you," or "Please make an appointment with my secretary," are examples of the intimidating language and actions that wear thin on people. These actions are not facilitative. They contain what could be looked upon as *hidden power*. The manager should just go to the employee and begin talking about whatever it is that needs to be talked about, or tell the employee what needs to be talked about and arrange a place to meet. To make an employee go through the formality of signing up with a secretary for a needed talk is to exude power. This is just an example of the forces that can be so well hidden in many institutions that wallow in the power-laden, top-down approach. They affect productivity, morale, motivation, learning, and the general attitudes of employees toward the company. It is a type of oppression unseen unless a person is working in a company.

One interesting example of poor management involved a manager who, by his own written words, suggested that he might not have faith in his staff to do the right thing. By judging them, he set himself up as a superior person.

Using the above-mentioned hidden power, he wrote a reminder to his staff that stated, "We are expecting twelve visitors for lunch today. They are coming in from various companies. Please be gracious."

Of course, employees could take this language to mean that the boss does not believe that members of his staff have the capacity to "be gracious." It could imply they have not been gracious in the past; that the boss knows how to be gracious, and the staff members do not. Above all else, it delivers the message that the manager does not trust his staff to do the right thing. This affects energy and spirit. It reveals the type of attitude that the manager has in working with people, and shows how he sees people in terms of their worth.

On occasion, some companies will take action to recognize employees, such as sending them to an athletic event and having their names put up on the electronic, computerized scoreboard to give them recognition. Although this special action could never take the place of eliminating spirit-killing language that goes on everyday, it helps to convey a caring attitude for a while. Employees like to feel that their work is appreciated and that their jobs are secure, but too many of the special actions of today are designed to gloss over the intimidation and fear generated by management behind closed doors.

America's businesses and industry could benefit by having a better understanding of the psychological aspects of work. The psychological ramifications that influence the well being of our country are being trivialized by business and government leaders. They are being trivialized to the extent that people are rebelling in terms of violence, apathy, and disdain for a government that has not put its finger on the real cause of disenchantment in the poor, the working class, the middle class, and to some extent the upper middle class. Employee and management relations will always have psychological overtones for business and government. For business, they will be in terms of productivity; for government, they will be in terms of who gets elected.

The quandary for both business and government is that the special language and special actions are missing from most companies in America, yet most companies advertise that they care about employees. Saying they care and showing they care are two different things. It used to be in the United States that caring about the employee was important, but now there is a widespread inability of management to show it consistently. In many cases, the company philosophy has changed so that social connectiveness is not important to top management.

The government has not taken any action that would lead those in the American workforce to believe that it fully understands Maslow's needs ladder, intrinsic motivation, the special language, and other factors that would help in motivating people throughout the country. It is almost like the government does not care how people are treated as long as businesses give the impression that they are solvent and they contribute to the campaign treasure chests of those who perpetuate the type of motivation going on in our businesses. Government seems to have the typical short-term outlook to which business has clung; it avoids the recent (and past) research that could give the United States a sound plan for the business world well into the twenty-first century.

Laws and regulations and investigative agencies are created by local, state, and federal governments to make the workplace motivational, but the attitude has always been that it is more important to cater to companies than to pay attention to the psychological needs of workers. Management and government have always had the cart in front of the horse when it comes to figuring out why businesses suffer, become mediocre, or sometimes even have to go out of business. They do not understand that an unhappy workforce, tired of the spirit killers, *subconsciously* helps to bring down a company or make it mediocre.

It is likely that sometime in the twenty-first century, business will be faced with its biggest dilemma ever. It will have to return to meeting the needs of America's citizens or it will not be allowed to operate without heavy-handed, specific regulations. It does not seem at this point in our history that business, like a delinquent parent, will be able to change itself to meet the needs of people other than just the corporate board members, CEOs, and shareholders.

These heavy-handed, specific regulations will first involve mandated management training programs that include such topics as motivation, encouragement, human relations, personality theory, and interpersonal communications. These might be taught through business schools at universities or local training stations. Surveys of worker contentment will be continuous.

Beyond the training aspect, business is probably going to force the hand of government, which is supposed to be *by the people and for the people*. This means that companies will have a choice of implementing a special language and special actions for motivation or be forced to change if they want to do business as it should be done—psychologically sound. The government of America and for Americans will, sometime in the twenty-first century, not be allowed to sit back and watch corporate America neglect the research that is leading to the slow deterioration of our country.

Change the Hierarchy—Change Manager Development

As alluded to in Chapter 2, several studies have shown that workers' perceptions of a manager are quite different form the manager's perception of himself. They know his style, whether he does or not. His effect on them is what they say it is. In our institutions as they are run today, if the effect is not good and the employees relay that message to management, they will either be harassed, fired, or transferred. Seldom does top-down management take such hints of mismanagement seriously.

These false beliefs managers have about their styles are well ingrained into the hierarchy. They are brought about by the boss believing that he has learned well from the "experts" on the way up the corporate ladder. If he is effective in the eyes of those above him in the hierarchy, that is all that counts. This self-deception, or we might say corporate deception, is an integral part of the traditional top-down, power-filled management system so prevalent in America today. It is not working near as well as it once did and will soon run out of steam. This deception is just another of our well-known cop-outs designed to keep the hierarchy system alive.

Training systems for business management in America produce managers whose attitudes and communication skills are contrary to good human development and contrary to the much-neglected research. We can now develop programs to reverse this costly trend, but businesses, colleges, and government must work together. This togetherness is a long way off in the future, but will eventually have to come to fruition. In ways not yet seen, the American people will see to it that they have more input into their standard of living and the conditions under which they work to maintain it.

Part of the problem with manager development today is that if they are not trained in an authoritarian way, the new recruits in the business world, anxious to please the top-down hierarchy, quickly develop autocratic methods to manage people. They do not have a choice.

The United States government has never had much input into business training systems involving management. The solvency of our businesses is so important to us as a nation that they have been given tremendous latitude in developing our people. They have almost every right to mismanage and de-motivate people, and then get rid of these people because they are not productive. It is unfortunate that the competitive global economy has put so much pressure on businesses that they have shown disdain for the psychological aspects of work. It is also unfortunate that the government is bewildered as to what to do about it.

Those who own small businesses or are a part of the hierarchy of a larger one see the government as interfering with their rights when the government makes too many laws and regulations that limit their functioning. The working class sees government as catering to businesses and infringing on their rights as spelled out under the Constitution.

It is somewhat of a mystery that government sticks its nose into some aspects of business, but not into others. For example, the Federal government diligently investigated popular Chicago restaurants for their claims about low-fat dishes. If the fat content of the servings did not meet the criteria as advertised to the general public, the restaurants were told to make the proper changes or face government sanctions. American workers might appreciate such a diligent monitoring of the workplace that is advertised as worker friendly, but is actually a hostile environment. Is investigating fat content more important than increasing worker morale?

Secretary of Labor under President Clinton, Robert Reich, said:

> There are those who treat workers as assets to be developed, while others treat workers as costs to be cut.[28]

Secretary Reich recognized the problem of how workers are treated, but so far no significant changes have been made in the workplace, and no investment in the future is assured by management changing its attitudes or by government monitoring.

Those interested in America's future should be able to see that the motivation and development of our people has become political. The two major parties, Democrat and Republican, have developed theories about how best to keep America operating, which include keeping businesses and schools strong and strengthening the family unit. It is an unfortunate situation that neither party is close to assuring that America will be vibrant throughout the twenty-first century.

Both political parties know that in a free market, tax-collecting form of government, it is important to distribute the wealth to those who live under it. The Democrats have controlled Congress for most of the last forty years.

They are known to be liberal in their thinking. They developed programs over the years that created what was known as the "welfare state," where millions of people did not work, but instead received checks from the government. Such programs put millions of people into poverty and demotivated American citizens by making them dependent on something other than themselves. The cost of this demotivation became so burdensome that America could no longer provide basic needs to millions of its people. It was psychologically unsound. Laws had to be enacted to force people to work. Bankruptcies occurred more often than in Depression years.

The Republicans, on the other hand, mostly conservative in their thinking, wrongly believe that business enterprises in America should govern themselves with little or no government interference. This theory, they believe, will unleash businesses so they can prosper and, with the compassion that business has for working men and women, our future will be secured. The problem with this theory is that business is no longer compassionate. It has become greedy.

An example of the Republican method of trying to get the best out of our people occurred when they took over Congress in the mid-1990s. They tried to pass bills which would limit the amount of regulations that government could impose on businesses, with the idea that this would create money for more jobs and higher wages. As their theory goes, the bigger the pie grows, the more there is to share. They believed that, with less regulations, corporate management would see to it that workers would get their "fair share." Many of the bills were vetoed by the Democrats because the American workforce sent the message that it no longer trusted management to share the pie. People had enough of working hard and seeing unfair shares of profits going to top management.

Such foolhardy programs that shrink government intervention while believing in the compassion of American management to create good jobs for the American worker are psychologically unsound because they perpetuate the abuse of power already causing chaos in America's institutions. The Republican theory is sound on paper, but not in practice.

Government should not have to intervene into companies that have the lifestyle of employees as a primary goal. Workers easily pick up on what is fair as well as what the government does not do to make management treat them fairly. Fair distribution of profits is essential in a democracy.

We should now recognize that capitalism carried to a greedy extreme is not a virtue that assists in the development of America.

The problems America faces in the twenty-first century in terms of being competitive have been brought on by the lack of understanding by both political parties as to how to get the best out of our people. Government must ensure that hardworking Americans who help companies earn large profits share in those profits to help ensure the basic needs of security, gratification, recognition, and self-esteem. Not until corporations fully understand that they are the backbone of the country and have direct input into the violent, need-depriving society in which we now live will America ever be the country it once was where people looked out for each other. Once companies catch on, optimal motivation is possible. Productivity will increase, and money will become available to those willing to work. Welfare programs will be a thing of the past.

Politics is as much a culprit in our problem of people development as any institution. To guarantee America's future, government and business (and education) leaders must rededicate themselves to understanding what the research in business psychology and organizational psychology, motivation, human relations, and other important areas of human development is telling us. Once there is agreement, there is a chance we can save ourselves from the neglect of the past by putting understanding leaders into power.

Government intervenes in dictating curriculum and accountability in our elementary and secondary schools, so why not dictate human development and motivational techniques to businesses? It is because corporate America is holding the government hostage because it believes it must have free reign to dispose of people or hire people to get the best the country has to offer. America cannot continue to function as well as it has in the past under such a belief that is based on an unsound way to develop people. Corporate America should not give up on people as quickly as it does.

It is likely that well into the twenty-first century, the government will have to force the hand of American business and demand more in return in terms of what business does for people and the communities in which they live.

The shortsightedness of American business was clearly seen in the 1990s when downsizing became the way to supposedly reenergize business and generate profits which, according to capitalistic theory, would be shared with all concerned in the business endeavor. Dr. Alan Downs, an industrial psychologist, helped perform many downsizings, and then wrote a book explaining why such hierarchical action did not work. The title of the book was almost as alarming as its contents: *Corporate Executions: The Ugly Truth About Layoffs—How Corporate Greed Is Shattering Lives, Companies, and Communities.*

In the book, which must be considered part of the research business is neglecting, Dr. Downs stated,

> The rules and assumptions about reduction that have been integrated into the bureaucratic paradigm are dangerously faulty. These assumed truths have permitted business leaders to make uncritical cuts in businesses that are in desperate need of rejuvenation, not dismemberment.[29]

Note that Dr. Downs observed that businesses need "rejuvenation," and we can be sure, based on the research, that the rejuvenation must come in terms of management practices. Spirit killing must end.

The book Dr. Downs wrote should be still another clue to the business world and the government that things are not working as well as advertised regarding the American workplace.

Life in the workplace for all Americans—management and nonmanagement, blue collar or white collar—is deteriorating. Everyone seems to be losing ground at an alarmingly fast pace.[29]

Dr. Downs' book clarified that layoffs are not good for the following reasons:

- Business profits
- Productivity in the future
- National economic stability

Greed, he explained, is the driving force, and it must be checked. Interestingly, he advocates a "new social contract" between companies and employees. This fits with the "social connectiveness" theory advocated by psychologists that would make companies worker friendly.

It seems as though we are so accustomed to our methods of management and motivation that we accept them even as our institutions become less effective. The decline in harmony in our institutions is not going to be recognized as a problem until far more people say it is a problem. It will be a certain number of influential people who will eventually make the difference.

We make laws that govern us, and we can change them; but a stubborn hierarchical system exists, beginning in Congress, and progressing into state legislatures. It is sad. It progresses all the way down to the homeless, hungry person sleeping in a cardboard box and to our children, millions of whom live in poverty. Government bodies are perhaps the worst in regard to top-down management.

The Japanese have claimed better working relationships with government and business than those found in the United States. If this is true, this cultural difference could again pay dividends for Japan if it follows the human development research that America has neglected. If Japan (or other countries) take note that all of our reengineering, restructuring, and downsizing is an excuse to hide our inability to get the best out of our people, then turn those notes into something that reenergizes their people, they could have another economic boom. The United States economy may not be able to withstand another onslaught, another boom from Japan or some other country.

A few companies are beginning to realize that manager development and the hierarchical top-down attitude promote mismanagement. They are moving ahead in management circles by making subtle and novel changes that promote a more intimate atmosphere. For example, United Airlines employees bought the company after management and labor strife nearly wrecked it. The employees now determine policy and working conditions.

A few companies have recognized that it is essential to tie in employee production with company profits. As a result, more companies are promoting the idea that employees should become shareholders as part of a benefit–profit sharing package. This will probably be the wave of the future once all of the dust clears that is stirring around today's mismanagement. A reasonable wage can be paid, and workers can use shares held as retirement funds for health care. Plans like this restrict the rigid flow of power and can help eliminate class distinctions among workers and management. It enhances respect for one person from another. However, it must be remembered the sharing of stock is an external motivation, and management will still run into problems if it does not concern itself with getting rid of the spirit killers and with instilling intrinsic motivation in its employees.

If manager development is to be restructured and the hierarchy toppled, it must be understood that a rigid structure is not necessary to control the behavior of people. One thing about management relying on self-reliance in employees is that those employees who are lazy and trying to get paid for not working hard will stick out like flies in a bowl of soup. Other employees, not management, soon develop ways to let these people and management know that they are not pulling their weight. It is a different story when management is responsible for widespread demotivation and disenchantment. Management has a more difficult time picking out the slackers when everyone is slacking because of power-driven managers.

Every Right to Mismanage

Besides developing managers who understand how to diffuse power, we must produce managers who understand that human rights and fairness are of primary importance. The rights that American citizens are supposed to have are so well advertised around the world that American citizens now, more than ever before, fight for those rights to be restored when they are infringed upon. It is unfortunate that employees are accustomed to leaving their rights in the company parking lot. They leave psychological needs there, too.

Hierarchies and a government that caters to them have given those who manage businesses every right to *mismanage,* and employees little right to *miswork.* Even basic rights, such as freedom of speech, freedom to assemble, and freedom from age, sex, and racial discrimination are overlooked even more often than the greed that is driving business leaders today.

Congress has had before it a bill that would allow corporations to replace workers who go on strike. No bill has ever come before Congress designed to replace misinformed, power-abusing management.

The right-to-work and the right-to-strike laws have, in fact, seen little enforcement because the government has chosen to make unions weak. The Caterpillar Company in Peoria, Illinois replaced workers in a bitter, long strike, and the government did not intervene in favor of the replaced workers. (Only Montana has laws that make employers deal fairly with employees.)

The Age Discrimination in Employment Act is something that most companies work around by cleverly designed intimidation programs. The government should be ashamed that it makes such laws, and then helplessly watches as they are abused. Seniority and experience on the job does not mean anything to management or, evidently, to our government because older workers have been dismissed in record numbers in the last two decades. Any hierarchy that loses an age discrimination suit is really in bad shape because about all it needs to say is, "His division was eliminated through downsizing." Group age discrimination seems to be OK with Washington, even though America loses some of its most valuable workers.

Courts are also filled with First Amendment cases in which workers tried to speak out about public concerns, but were retaliated against by vindictive administrations. Many business officials know they can get away with firing someone on the spot; or, if that seems too risky for a good, long-employed worker who speaks out, involuntary transfers are popular. If that fails to get employees to resign, cases are quickly built against them where evaluations of their work are rigged. The employee suddenly is not doing a good job, is released, or becomes so discouraged that he resigns in hopes of finding gainful employment elsewhere. Sexual harassment on the job is just beginning to get the attention it deserves. It is alarming in America that companies can now take advantage of laws that allow them to spy on employees.

No matter what the charges are that an employee brings against an employer, the courts in America currently give an employee little chance to defend himself. The burden of proof is often insurmountable. Many employees who have been attacked do not bother to fight back because legal help is too costly. The courts and government officials have to know that rights are for sale in America; they are not guaranteed as the Constitution implies.

It is sad that only a few of America's dedicated workers have the finances and the courage to fight the big money and the expert law firms. It is clear that the hierarchical power structure, like an amoeba, has slithered into a cozy position in the justice system. The injustices the hierarchy has perpetuated through the courts have become spirit killers that will linger into the twenty-first century.

In Illinois alone, one federal appeals court decision in the 1980s should be enough to tell working America where it stands with its government. The Illinois Department of Human Rights dismissed 5500 civil rights claims in the late 1970s and early 1980s. The University of Chicago Law School's Mandel Legal Aid Clinic filed suit in the United States District Court in Chicago alleging that the procedures the Illinois Department of Human Rights used to investigate employment discrimination claims were unfair. The federal appeals court ruled that even though the Illinois agency *violated constitutional principles* of these workers, it did not require the agency to reinvestigate the 5500 claims because it would be too costly. The decision saved the state of Illinois millions of dollars.

Anyone remotely interested in establishing fairness in the workplace would have to reject this decision, which means that convenience of government is more important than civil rights. It is a typical example of top-down management running roughshod over Americans who are asked to give their all for their country. *Even government has the right to mismanage.* It is little wonder that only about half of the registered voters do vote.

There are so many spirit killers, including those in the legal system, lurking in American institutions today that it is remarkable we have survived as well as we have. In some respects we are fortunate, as the signals are telling us that management techniques must change and the judicial system can help change them.

The media has helped some in informing workers about their rights, but most workers are not aware of what an authoritarian workplace can get away with to make life miserable for them. Many authoritarian institutions actually encourage managers to infringe on the rights of workers because they see this as motivational. One large institution in the Chicago area was forced to go to court over a First Amendment violation. Testimony revealed that management was told not to put "anything positive, all negatives" in an evaluation of an employee who had spoken out on some issues of public concern. The same management, when interviewing people for administrative positions, was known to ask, "Do you have any objections to building cases against people?" Predictably this institution has had five civil law suits filed against it in the last decade, but the government has not been very active in eliminating such tyranny from it. The institution finally proclaimed that it had become "unapproachable" to employees.

Part of the intent of the insulting, top-down theory is to create a chilling effect. If many workers see only a few getting intentionally designed harassment, everyone will keep their noses to the grindstone, and productivity will, as the theory goes, stay at a good level. Those who view the atrocities usually do not have the courage to put their jobs on the line and speak out, so the hierarchical management assumes all is going well because no one is reporting that things are not going well. Such disillusioned mismanagement is common in institutions in the United States.

The ability to silence people, to create a chilling effect, is currently a skill admired in most hierarchies, but it is a major reason why so many experience difficulties as they try to compete with the competition. No originality comes forth, and little thinking is going on. Policies are made by top management, and any disagreement could end a worker's career.

To plug up the loopholes that now give management every right to mismanage, the legislative bodies, the judges and juries of the future, may have to muster some courage and rule that many old, precedent-setting cases were based on erroneous beliefs about how management should morally and ethically be allowed to treat America's workforce. If any segment of our society is contributing to the poor development of people within our society, an investigation should be made as to how that misinformed segment can make an acceptable contribution. Such decisions involving the workers of America can no longer be based on convenience of government or on neglecting the research telling us how to best develop our people.

The friction, discouragement, and diminished spirit that mismanagement causes promulgates the time-wasting litigation that always diminishes morale and productivity. Management could cut down considerably on the time and money spent on legal hassles by spending more time on implementing effective forms of motivation and communication.

The devastation that the top-down approach brings when it infringes on or denies workers their Constitutional rights or rights to work are frequently winked at by the government. To use lies and deceit when writing up an evaluation of a worker, or to transfer a worker to an unwanted position to discourage him, is perhaps the lowest form of illegal labor practices, but such practices are common. What has happened to our moral fiber? In a court of law, the lies and deceit are often looked upon as an "opinion" of the boss, and the courts often accept the well-designed deceit of any corporation. The problem is, even if laws are passed to protect the work force, management is quick to figure out how to circumvent them.

In today's America, age discrimination is common as middle-aged men with families suffer layoffs from companies making record profits. Younger, less expensive workers are then hired, and the government often sees this as keeping the company viable. Those outside the government, those looking to the future, see this as contributing to the cause of the tension gripping our nation. This tension causes us to be among the leaders in drug use throughout the world. The United States is now looked upon as a country where violence is a major issue that was hardly thought about forty years ago.

Seldom is our drug culture attributed to the way people are treated in our institutions. The tension within people has to be created from some source, and more than likely that source is created by unsettled conditions in the environment.

American citizens deserve and want a safer environment, but the casual approach the government takes to research that tells us we should do things differently in developing people is distressing at best. It is mismanagement at the highest level.

Whipping people into shape, climbing someone's frame, dressing down, reading the riot act to the rank and file, to the troops, and to those in the salt mines or to those in the trenches, are common phrases known in the workplace in America. They reflect the attitude involved in the top-down approach to management. The attitude is hindering our development as a nation because it allows our traditional past, which is supported by the government, corporate America, and our judicial system, to keep new management techniques at bay.

The United States Postal Service has been an interesting study in top-down management. The circumstances surrounding it should be another clue that could help us determine what changes need to be made in management to make future generations prosper from our decisions.

Following a shooting in the Royal Oak, Michigan post office, where a fired postal worker killed four managers, a report was compiled by the congressional General Accounting Office. The report, launched by two Senators, revealed tension-filled working conditions and relationships at several postal locations.

The GAO discovered that problems were related to an "autocratic management style." Workers were frustrated because they felt managers did not "value their input" on how to organize and accomplish their work.

It was noted that the U.S. Postal Service suffers from a "dysfunctional organizational culture." The two-volume report was titled, *U.S. Postal Service: Labor–Management Problems Persist on the Workroom Floor.*

The government report about the country's postal service revealed that "management's traditional attitude has been that workers respond best, and perhaps only, to discipline." Notice the word *traditional* is used. The alarming thing about such a report is, why does the government believe this dysfunctional management style is limited to the postal service? Research has told us for years that such mismanagement is common in a great majority of our institutions.

The attitude of the government seems to be that because the postal service is a function of government to serve people, it must be changed; but the private sector can go right on treating workers in a similar dysfunctional manner. It does not make sense until we look at business lobbyists who contribute heavily to elected officials to sway their votes to keep government out of the way of business so corporations can do what they want with people. Government trusts business too much to do the right things to meet the needs of America's workers. The hands-off policy is setting up a situation that will become explosive sometime in the twenty-first century.

It is not only alarming, but also discouraging to the American worker that the federal government uses research when it wants to and disregards it when it wants to.

The government constantly bombards us with research and ads telling us how the use of drugs is dragging down our nation to the tune of billions of dollars and unprecedented violence. It is unlikely that a government report will be presented to the public stating that research shows that dysfunctional management in the postal service is no different from the dysfunctional management in most of our institutions. Such a report would not be politically correct for those elected officials standing behind the report who need money from big business to get reelected.

The above case scenario is presented to help show how mismanagement in most institutions in the United States is swept under the rug. It is a big mistake for the future of America for the government to continue to turn its back on the American worker by neglecting research regarding management and human development. To do so allows our institutions to continue dysfunctional management practices that create an environment not conducive to productivity. Such an attitude promotes mini-dictatorships that are ineffective and often explosive.

If asked, some managers might tell us that good management is the process of meeting goals and objectives through the effective influencing of people. In reality, power has replaced influence in the United States in almost all walks of life. It should be obvious that there is a wide gap in thinking as to how people are most effectively motivated and how they are motivated in the United States.

America Cannot Change Its Culture, But It Can Make Changes

Changing century-old beliefs, customs, social values, mores, and other aspects of a society can rarely, if every, be accomplished. These changes do not seem necessary to make the changes needed in America's autocratic, top-down approach to developing its people. Just because something is old and traditional and treated with reverence, like our hierarchy system, does not mean it is right for a developing country. Two researchers looking into organizational relationships agreed that changes would not come easy in the business world. Richard Pascale and Anthony Athos said,

> There is no quick fix in sight. Rather each company's CEO and other top executives need to recognize that it takes time, discomfort, stamina, and commitment to strengthen what is weak in their organizational development.[24]

They added, "Mechanistic, programmatic solutions that do not change what executives do and, indeed, to some degree who they are, are likely to fail."[24] It should be added that people for whom these executives are responsible must be involved in the organizational development because people like to have input into those decisions that have impact upon them.

Note that these researchers previously mentioned that, in order for management to change for the better, the changes might have to go deep enough not only to change what executives do, but also to "some degree who they are." Does not this mean an attitude change? Do those who want to be effective managers of the future have to consider changing traditional beliefs about how to motivate people? Such changes are for certain, and only time will tell if the changes are made voluntarily or as a result of some sort of turmoil. If past decisions by the government and business are any indication, the changes will not be voluntary; they will be made because of a crisis situation stemming from how people are motivated.

If America is to move forward in productivity, management must learn that no ideas are wrong and no one can overachieve. It is impossible to overachieve, yet this term is in the media constantly and is accepted by most people. People cannot do any more than they are capable of doing. Calling someone an overachiever may be a put down. It attacks their original worth. All of us have more of a capacity to accomplish things than we or others realize.

It is possible to underachieve. We have many Americans underachieving because a hierarchical system at home, school, or work discourages them so much that they do not want to set goals and accomplish even those things they are capable of doing. Those who achieve great things have worked around, within, through, and over our system of motivation. The system should not make it so difficult for people to achieve things they are capable of doing.

Since we cannot change our entire culture, we must change the people within it who are making decisions that limit the motivation of people. It is now imperative, before we get too far into the twenty-first century, that drastic changes come from our executives, those at the top of the corporations, organizations, and agencies, including government, so they can become better leaders. Many have, as the research has revealed, been misinformed about motivational theories.

Radical surgery on emotions that will transplant more empathy must be performed on the strong personalities of these leaders. Corporations would be wiser to downsize or makeover or reengineer top leaders, instead of downsizing the entire fleet of workers. A makeover to a more congenial, less power-oriented form of leadership would soon bring the improved results that research infers would happen.

Cultures develop circumstances within them that require change when those things that have worked in the past are no longer working. Thomas Jefferson believed that any society needed dramatic change from time to time. In order for America to compete in the twenty-first century and be a world leader, it must influence leaders not only to change things they are accustomed to doing, but also to change their thinking in terms of how they go about getting the best effort out of people.

We cannot change our culture, but we must change perceptions within our culture as to just what businesses can do legally in terms of getting around meeting the needs of people. Early in our history, it seemed to be an unwritten law that institutions were to be social in nature and, like it or not, they should only be allowed to exist within the culture if they met the needs of people. One thing is for certain as we approach the next century: more compassion among people will be needed to ensure our survival.

One example of compassion disappearing in American business is the arrival of the temporary worker. Companies try to work around meeting the needs of employees by hiring temporary workers for whom they do not have to provide medical insurance or pensions. These benefits, common practice in our nonviolent, drug-free days, are a form of security, the most basic of all needs. Does the hiring of temporary workers and the loss of medical care and pensions indicate that we are losing the competition wars to other countries? If so, should not leaders in our organizations take a look at what has caused us to lose this security blanket and, instead of making things worse for America's people, find a solution? If we are not losing the competition battle to other countries, then greed must, as many suspect and profit reports show, be the reason why so many Americans are losing the security blanket that past leaders seem so able to supply.

Another clue that compassion is a thing of the past in our culture is the fact that American businesses are moving to other countries. This is a radical development in our history, but it is taking place. A few brave and proud corporations that believe in America are taking steps to change the workplace that is limiting their productivity so they can stay home. Many are going about it in the wrong way by not looking at management first; but by starting a process, they may find answers before competition in the next century sweeps them away.

We have too many people running away from problems in America. Now the corporations we need to keep us strong are running away instead of checking up to see why they cannot make the profits here that they would be making by moving. Of course, one of the answers given by top management is that labor costs too much in the United States. American management may want to consider that motivation is the same for all people in the world.

If American corporations move to other countries and begin their top-down management practices, they will soon discover that people will figure out they are not being treated fairly; then productivity will decrease. Sometime in the twenty-first century, this moving away will backfire on American management, and business will be back to square one. One former employee of a large American corporation called this "circular progress." Running around in circles and trying to find out how to stay ahead of competition is something American management should be used to by now.

The United States has been the most profitable culture in the world, but other countries have improved their technology and are moving closer to us in their ability to produce goods and increase the standard of living for people. Since motivation of the human being is the same around the world, our leaders must begin to realize that if we do not stay ahead in this area of human development, our culture may not be able to participate in the world markets of the twenty-first century as well as we did in the twentieth century. At the very least, it seems risky to avoid solving this problem.

From Research to Mediocrity or Excellence?

We are now to the point in our long history where research has revealed that something is drastically wrong with our business community and the processes it often uses to get results from people.

The psychological assessment of our culture in regard to how we develop our people is complete, and the diagnosis, as well as the prognosis, is not good.

Feeble attempts have been made to overcome the debilitating effects of our denial of the research on human development. For example, when our system of management and the resulting productivity lag first became evident, some companies understood that solutions rested with people inside the institution. The result was that management quickly appropriated money for Human Resource and Development (HRD) departments to monitor problems.

By giving life to HRD, the hierarchy simply meant that people other than those at the top of the organization needed to take a look at themselves and see how they could become more productive. This attitude prevails today. To management, answers to lagging productivity in quantity and quality needed to be found somewhere below the top of the organization. Top management, as usual, assumed it could not possibly have anything to do with the poor motivation causing the productivity lag.

Although HRD departments are a good idea if used properly, they are a cruel illusion in most companies, a facade and an unconscious deception that contributes to the hierarchy system maintaining the status quo.

Workers and executives alike are mesmerized into thinking that if a large amount of money is appropriated, the company is showing it cares, and something good will happen for the workers to increase their productivity. Seldom does a change in management practices occur. Primary concentration is focused on everything but breaking down the powerful pyramid. The top must give the middle and the bottom of the pyramid permission, not just money, to investigate and implement change—and that includes changes in management.

Human Resource and Development departments cannot facilitate change without an admission from the top that the addiction to power is hurting the company. In order to increase productivity, the HRD people must be effective enough to recognize those forces that kill the spirit of people and how these forces diminish their desire to work hard. They must be courageous and skillful enough in counseling top management to give up the nation's most powerful drug—power. In most companies, the HRD departments have nearly become part of the hierarchy because the fear of telling top management that it is killing the spirit of workers runs deep. It is part of the chilling effect that most hierarchies have built up for themselves.

Not so astonishing, most HRD departments do not know how to teach management to give up the power and become more effective. They need expertise in implementing a more encouraging, special language and an understanding that true motivation is brought about by improved interpersonal communication and by diffusing power.

Through the years, other attempts have been made to promote togetherness that labor and management so urgently need in our society. Quality circles, empowering workers, and participatory management were programs designed to make the workplace more harmonious, but they turned out to be the common lip-service that management in a rigid pyramid gives out.

The research into how to manage and motivate people is so conclusive that more studies should not have to be done. We have been shown what needs to be done to get better results from our people, but too many people who could influence the change are not cooperating.

Dr. Thomas Gordon made a gallant effort when he wrote *L.E.T.—Leader Effectiveness Training* in 1977. On the first page of that informative book, he reveals that research has, indeed, handed to us the ingredients needed to make American management the best in the world. It remains an unsolved mystery in America why the research has not been applied to something that is so important to a developing nation. Dr. Gordon stated,

Now that much of the mystery has been taken out of the concept of leadership, it is possible to describe rather precisely what it takes to be an effective leader. The thousands of studies enable us to build a model of leader effectiveness based on solid research evidence from many types of organizations and groups.[20]

Referring to his book, Dr. Gordon stated,

It is one of the purposes of this book to bring that model out of the privacy of university laboratories into the public domain, where it will be easily accessible to the countless people who find themselves in positions of leadership . . . in government, in business and industrial organizations, in schools, in families.[20]

One of the purposes of this book is to show how the research Dr. Gordon discusses, as well as the research and writings of countless others who have explored leadership, has been neglected.

By Dr. Gordon's account, one might think that we have solved the problem of management motivating people correctly, and that management skills are clear and precise. He is correct, but despite his efforts and the plethora of research, a unified effort has never been made to change management practices in the United States.

If we are to use the "thousands of studies" and move to excellence instead of staying at a nonoptimal level of productivity in the twenty-first century, we must realize that compassion from management to labor must take high priority. Only a few managers or owners of companies have understood the importance of this concept. Following are a few examples that are important to consider for future motivation of the workforce.

When owner Arron Feuerstein's plant burned to the ground in Massachusetts and his workers had no place to go for work, he told them not to worry. He told his colleagues that they all would be paid and that they would rebuild the company together. He made a "social connection," a commitment to his workers, that he would help take care of them since they had been so good to him in building up the company. Such compassion is rare in American business today, but is something that we will need more of in the future.

The *Chicago Sun-Times* published a story titled, "One Company's Amazing Road to Labor Peace." The story told about one CEO whose philosophy encouraged workers to trust him. Even though he did his best to

manage the company based on the philosophy, the labor/management relations had deteriorated badly. The manager's trust broke down and he knew
the workers would not trust words; so he figured he had to come up with another way of communicating.

Just when things looked as though they were going to be totally out of control, the CEO finally stated, "Whatever demands the official committee of the
union drew up, they would all be accepted automatically. One hundred percent."

The CEO in the above situation decided that all demands, such as coming
to work late, leaving early, or going out during the work day, would be left up
to the workers. He took the time to talk with every employee and explain his
reasoning.

He said, "I'm not doing this to make you trust me. I'm doing it so that you
know that you are trusted."

Whatever demands the workers made were fine. In fact, the CEO told the
workers if they wanted to be paid a large salary and dissolve the company, that
would be accepted. He decided that workers were only working at about 40
percent of their capacity while they could be working at 80 percent, and something needed to be done.[30]

The change was drastic, but the company still prospers. The change shows
several things about management, labor, and productivity. When unquestioned trust is present, a high level of productivity will prevail. Unquestioned
trust does not exist in the current organizational structure of America's corporations. Besides trust, the experiment also showed that people will govern
themselves, and peer pressure is far more effective than management pressure.
This expression of trust by the CEO cultivated reciprocal trust on the part of
the workers and kept the business going.

Too many companies in America, in which trust has broken down, are still
spending what could be productivity time on trying to keep unions out or trying to break those already in place. Some companies, the good companies,
have been so effective in motivating people and meeting their needs that
workers say a union is not necessary.

Unions are formed to be watchdogs so management will be fair in its treatment of employees. We know the government has not been a good watchdog
since rights have become so expensive to purchase and cannot be pursued
with the money that average workers make.

Part of the problem with motivation in America is that unions have become hierarchies in themselves. Often members pay dues and are promised
comprehensive legal assistance only to find out they are not protected from
retaliation by a vindictive employer. It is sad that the United States Supreme
Court has ruled that "unions must back their constituents." In a mockery of

American justice, the Illinois Appeals Court ruled that "unions have no obligation" to back their constituents[31]. Again, the lack of enforcement of laws on the books caters to a system of management that is being questioned worldwide.

If we believe in the research that reveals that mismanagement is commonplace in the United States, many companies and other institutions must be on the brink of having unions organize against them. The organizing is done to balance the power, obtain needs, and fight for an improved work environment that would increase productivity and make everyone happy. Unions are caused; they do not just happen. They are strikes back against management that knows little about human development. To vote against a company and organize a union is to vote against today's methods of motivation . . . and the enforcement of civil rights laws.

Management victories gained by running roughshod over people taint our culture and our future. They use money that could be put to better use. They put a cloud over our once-proud reputation for motivation throughout the world. Today, business in the United States spends more money on union activities, including strikes, than any other country in the world.

In corporate America, why is it so difficult for people who want to play on the same winning team to figure out a way to meet the needs of everyone concerned? Is it that difficult to learn to speak in a more encouraging language, to give up power, to provide gratification, recognition, and security? It is imperative that this situation be remedied before the next century arrives.

The stress our autocratic style of developing people encourages is a major force that must be derailed as we plan for the future. The stress put on workers as well as management is caused by our spirit-killing motivational techniques. Some organizations have dealt with the symptoms rather than causes by developing Employee Assistance Programs. These programs are designed to treat those health problems partially caused by the tremendous amount of stress the autocratic management styles create. Medical reports tell us that stress causes many serious illnesses. Companies could easily cut the costs of treating these illnesses by implementing a more socially connected workplace. Some companies are paying for illnesses they help to create.

America is in the infancy stage of understanding how our spirit-killing words can cause stress and absenteeism. Medical doctors are well aware of stress produced on the job because they see many workers who complain of aches and pains for which there is no physical cause. Doctors can prescribe drugs to relieve the symptoms, but the cure for the effect of our spirit-killing words cannot be found in a doctor's office. The cure must be found within the organizational structure of the company.

Productivity can be improved dramatically by leaders who understand that high rates of drug and alcohol consumption, divorce, violence, suicides, and chronic illnesses are often promoted by tension-filled work environments. We fool ourselves if we believe that spirit-killing words, heard everyday by some workers, cannot lead to the above-mentioned afflictions that are very costly to our country. Companies that neglect current research and cling to traditional styles of management are destined to be plagued by stress-related inefficiency well into the twenty-first century.

The morale of employees is affected when they begin to share the notion that management is affecting their mental and physical health. Morale is even worse now that many companies do not want to pay for medical coverage. In autocratic managed institutions, for an employee to admit that stress has become a personal problem is to admit weakness. To admit weakness is, to a tough-minded, insensitive boss, the best way to be terminated.

Congress, state legislatures, and the courts can no longer use their interpretation of the research as an excuse to cater to corporations that run roughshod over America's workers. In order for us to avoid mediocrity and move efficiently from the research to excellence, it must be understood that a spiritual, humanistic, and intellectual reawakening must occur to replace top-down management. The transformation can be somewhat scientific in nature and even looked upon as a technology that will change the workplace for the better. This revitalization, this reenergizing, will result in more socially connected institutions that bring people together instead of tearing them apart.

The new technology means that management must take the reigns and create a more encouraging, intimate work environment. We were told this as far back as 1927, and have been reminded of it several times since. To maintain the status quo may make our future security elusive.

4 Top-Down Management in Education

Introduction

A lbert Einstein noted perceptively,

> It is in fact nothing short of a miracle that modern methods of instruction have not yet strangled the holy curiosity of inquiry. It is a very grave mistake to think that enjoyment of seeing and searching can be promoted by means of coercion and a sense of duty.

We have learned how the traditional, trial-and-error, top-down management style of motivation in business has strangled the initiative, originality, creativity, energy, and enthusiasm of workers. Research has informed us that we can no longer base motivation on power, fear, coercion, embarrassment, intimidation, retaliation, and humiliation. It is alarming to discover that Einstein, a high school dropout who later transformed the world of physics and won the Nobel Prize, agreed that similar, demotivational, spirit-killing forces are sadly entrenched in education.

It is traditional in the business world to ignore research and rely on a hierarchical structure that hinders progress in human development. This structure has been transferred to education. Such reliance is preventing America's educational institutions from even holding the status quo with many other countries. Now that the United States is in a transition from an industrial society to an information society, a lack of progress in education causes deterioration. Either education improves or atrophy will set in.

The discouraging, anti-inspirational forces, which can simply be defined as our inability to understand and implement sound motivational techniques, are devastating education. As with our workers, we are not getting the best out

117

of our students. Never before has a nation spent so much time spinning its wheels in an attempt to educate people. It is remarkable that there are leaders in the education hierarchies, just as in business, who say, "Why try to fix it if it is not broken." Others agree with Einstein that education is headed for a crisis if traditional methods of management and instruction are not totally reformed into a more motivational climate.

We blame the decline of education on excessive television viewing, poorly designed curriculums, underpaid teachers, short school years, and a host of other reasons. Just as in business management, we are experts at conjuring up reasons for not taking a strong, microscopic look at our methods of motivation in education.

In business enterprises in America, a serious flaw hinders productivity; such is also the case in education. Einstein thought so. So did another social observer, Bill Russell. He mentioned that during his school days, "teachers prepared kids for the harsh realities of the outside world by deflating their dreams with cynical comments."[32] Considering that which has been covered so far about motivation, encouragement, and human development, do we have difficulty believing that a teacher might try to motivate a student by making a cynical, spirit-killing remark such as, "the way you are going in math this year, you won't make graduation requirements"?

It is true. Fear, coercion, humiliation, embarrassment, intimidation, cynical comments, and other spirit killers wrongfully used in business are alive and well in education. They have been used so much in these American institutions that productivity in business and the lack of learning in education are two of the most discussed topics in American journalism. Leaders in business sit on school boards and help transfer the traditional, but ineffective forms of motivation into our schools. Administrators in education have always followed the lead of our all-important business world.

Several years ago, *U.S. News and World Report* ran a cover picture of a teacher with the caption, "What's Wrong with Our Teachers?" (Will we ever see a cover titled "What's Wrong with Our Managers"?) Things were progressing so slowly in educating our young people that the federal government stepped in and published the now famous *A Nation at Risk* report. This report and other sound educational research told us that education should concentrate on two major items if our desire is to increase learning. First, students need to spend more time on tasks in school. Second, instructors need to become more encouraging to their students. School management must see to it that these things are accomplished.

Remember the "halo effect," in which research in the business world revealed that people are more productive if they believe that someone cares about them? It is no different in our schools where educators must be more encouraging and caring if they are to help keep students on task, learning those things that are vital not only to their well being, but also to the future of America. A plethora of research in education has been neglected just as it has been in the business world. This neglect does not paint a pretty picture for our future.

Misinterpreted Research—Spirit Killers in Education

As in business and politics, there are not enough people in education who understand the ramifications of the vast amount of research compiled. The results are being misinterpreted by federal, state, and local education officials as well as most teachers and administrators. Following is an account of what has happened to put education in such disarray.

Soon after the federal Office of Education released the *A Nation at Risk* report, school officials across the country set up programs to remove the risks from the decaying educational process. Programs were designed to get students to study harder, which would satisfy the requirements to make students stay on task. Studies other than *A Nation at Risk* had earlier revealed that teachers should learn to be more encouraging.

The "time on task" concept meant to most educators that we needed to get tougher, more autocratic, and, essentially, do the same thing in education that the business world usually did when it needed to get people to be more productive. It was incorrectly assumed that fear would be a good motivator, along with our numerous other spirit-killing devices.

The "time on task" concept has become elusive because programs set up to help students meet this national goal were copied from programs designed to increase productivity in the business world. Such efforts failed miserably in the business world because they were organized from the top-down, authoritarian, might-is-right attitude that has never helped people develop their talents. In the management of education, as well as business, we failed to look at our traditional, impersonal motivational techniques. Instead of employing sound motivational practices, as research was telling us to do, we reverted to an even more hard-line, authoritarian approach in education than in business.

In order to help students stay on task and learn more, educators made them go to school longer, take more classes, pay more attention in classes, do more homework, and be more closely supervised in study halls. All of this was supposedly for the improvement of education, to secure our future so we would no longer be "at risk."

It is unfortunate that our coercion and sense of duty, our external methods of motivation, will put American education on hold as it enters the twenty-first century.

Those interested in improving education might ask, "How do we get off hold?" We might start where we noted business must start, by becoming better equipped to provide intrinsic motivation and encouragement to those we teach. In education, this getting off hold must start in our classrooms. We must look at our teachers as managers responsible for good human development.

Time on task must be improved rapidly in every school, and this can be done by looking at the intricate, subtle things that cause students to get off task in the first place. Students are supposed to work, so they might be compared to workers in the world of work. How do workers get off task? Keep in mind that America's workers have now become discouraged, their self-esteem is declining, and they do not feel a sense of pride or a part of the team in the corporate structure. Their energy and enthusiasm are on the decline. They do not feel appreciated or gratified. At times, even the basic need of security has been taken from them. Often their Constitutional rights are infringed upon. Many just say, "I do what I am told, and go home at five o'clock." The jobs hold no meaning for the employees. They do not think about being creative or loyal. The same attitudes have been instilled into a vast majority of the young people in our schools because the motivation there is similar to the motivation in the world of work.

Granted, things are a little different in a classroom or a hallway, a locker room or a school cafeteria, regarding the interaction of a student and a teacher as compared to an employee and a manager. But things are not as different as we would like to believe. Remember, good methods of motivation are the same for everyone.

To be more specific, in comparing motivation in education and business, recall the Western Electric research done in 1927. It revealed that people become more productive when they firmly believe that people under whom they are working really care about them as individuals. Recall also the human relations skills briefly described in Chapter 2. These skills are based on solid research done by human development experts over the last 60 to 70 years.

When these skills are not applied on a daily basis in the business world, productivity suffers. We know that a spirit-killing form of communication is solidly entrenched in the business world. The same applies to our educational institutions, and it has become devastating to the learning process.

America's teachers believe they care about their students, but research tells us that they are not able to show it. The care is not shown because too much power, authority, coercion, embarrassment, ridicule, humiliation, and a multitude of other spirit killers exists in our schools just as it does in workplaces. When the research-based human relations skills are missing from our classrooms, education suffers much more than is currently being recognized.

To get more specific about what happened to cause the decline in education, let us look at an important article from a progressive educational publication. The article, titled, "Low-Profile Classroom Controls," states that "conventional classroom controls are not working well for teachers today."[33] We know that conventional workplace controls are not working well for management either.

Conventional means traditional, something commonly used, something people are used to having around. "In short, conventional classroom controls are high-profile. They distract student's attention first, before focusing on lesson content," the article tells us. Statements that most Americans have heard in the classroom, such as, "All right, may I have your attention please?" or "We will simply have to wait until we have everyone's attention," are good examples of a high-profile teacher administering conventional classroom controls.[33]

It is obvious that such statements are a top-down approach to getting attention. We might ask, What's wrong with these statements? Specifically, they tend to get students off task or inattentive. "Look at me!" or "I want it quiet in here" are a couple of others mentioned in the article. Other requests for quiet are, "Why aren't you paying attention?" or "Stop fooling around and get to work," and "Sit up straight and pay attention."[33] Many of these comments are remarks that most Americans heard as they went through school.

We can see that the language is somewhat demanding, and a demeaning atmosphere is taking shape. It is difficult for those in education to recognize the effects that demanding, threatening, power-filled statements have on young people. These types of statements wear down students after a period of time, just as similar power-filled statements wear down America's workers.

Recall that the use of *I* signifies power, and "Why"-type questions will probably wear thin on people. Discouraging remarks and the inability to influence people without using force, coercion, fear, embarrassment, and humiliation, slowly causes workers and students to be less productive, to get off task. When inner needs are not met, workers and students alike will exercise their power to control how hard they work. Only minimum requirements are met when self-esteem and belongingness are affected.

In America today, we see our schools being mismanaged much the same way as our businesses are being mismanaged. Many of our top corporations are in trouble, or will be in the twenty-first century, simply because of the way they have developed their people. A chilling effect has paralyzed most of the business community because the top-down approach has not given people the opportunity to develop their talents. They are thrown off task by spirit-killing remarks from supervisors. This same type of management is hindering our schools. Students are not developing their talents to the fullest because they get off task as they become discouraged and disenchanted with a management system that uses a high-profile, autocratic approach to keep them on task.

Research in education not only shows that students must stay on task, but it also shows that our spirit-killing, discouraging remarks get them off task in the first place.

There is no difference, psychologically speaking, between why a worker does not put forth a better effort and why a student does not put forth a better effort. Both are motivated in the same way, and both are demotivated in the same way.

The high-profile language just mentioned and our spirit-killing words also interfere with the all-important "special language" being incorporated into the education community.

We now know that workers fight back against an autocratic language with a slackening of effort. Controlling the quality of their work becomes almost a game as does complaining fostered by the lack of gratification in and recognition of their work. Schools, also void of a more encouraging language, soon detect slackening efforts and discipline problems that cause poor quality in the work of students. Teachers are not as productive as they could be because the top-down, power-filled language is used by administrators and demotivates them as well.

Indifferent attitudes to the learning process are, unwittingly, promulgated by those who manage our schools and by teachers who use high-profile language to motivate. All of our institutions would function better if a low-profile form of speaking was used to motivate people. It is now as clear as a windshield on a new car that our number one problem in American education is how to make the schools more positive in their approach to developing our young people.

Of course, many adults in America say, "I made it through school, and it wasn't so bad." This is just one of many statements that help maintain the top-down approach our country traditionally follows in developing its people. It is another cop-out that keeps us mired in the status quo. Our failure to recognize this primary cause of the criticism of our educational system does, indeed, put America at risk.

Since the missing special language seems to be so much a culprit in education, especially in our classrooms and in discipline, let us look at it in more depth.

After being in a class for a few weeks, a student said to her counselor, "I don't like my science teacher." The student could not pinpoint just why she did not like her teacher. She did say, after thinking back, that her teacher had said to her in front of other students, "Are you not going to hand in a paper and just take an F like you did last time?" The student said to the counselor, "That did sort of turn me off a little."

The words spoken by the teacher upset the girl. The words were somehow punishing her and came across as a threat. They were designed to embarrass her in front of her classmates. It was the beginning of a deteriorating relationship. The words were high-profile, spirit diminishing, and demotivational. The unseen enemy had begun its work. The spirit killers had arrived. This is a classic example of how a teacher unintentionally began to instill resentment in the student.

The teacher in the above example is obviously frustrated with the student who is about to earn a second consecutive failing grade. A better, low-profile response would be, "Your paper was missing in the group checked last night. Do you plan to hand one in?" Who among us would deny that this a better remark? It is the beginning of instilling self-reliance in the student. This response does not come across to the student as a threat. The impetus for learning is left up to the student (as it always is), and the relationship between student and teacher stays intact.

By using the suggested response, the teacher refrains from falling into the traditional trap of using coercion, embarrassment, fear, and intimidation to get the student to hand in a paper. The teacher is careful not to use external motivation by mentioning grades. It is, and always will be, up to the student, not the teacher, to hand in a paper or not.

In attempting to teach the special language being recommended here, we might consider that we cannot make anyone do anything. If someone does not want to do something, he or she can probably avoid doing it. This is why using influence is better than using power. Power often does not work, whereas influence has a good chance. It may not be as swift, but the results of influence last longer and are more meaningful. In the student–teacher case just mentioned, the power was being switched on by the teacher, and the student was beginning to feel it. The relationship was headed toward deterioration. Situations such as this happen daily in every school, and learning suffers.

Motivational experts know that the key to promoting learning and self-disipline in our schools is to teach those who work in the schools how to give up power. Teachers, administrators, and other school personnel abuse their power just as managers do in the business world. The abuse of power kills the spirit, energy, and enthusiasm of young people, and these are difficult to regain.

Education is, by most accounts, in sad disarray. Young people, as the government has attested, are not on task and are not learning as they should. They strike back at an undemocratic school system just as workers do, with a slackening of effort. We might contribute this poor effort to Dr. Thomas Gordon's view of what happens when power is abused. Recall he said, "Perhaps it is inevitable that coercive power generates the very forces that eventually will combat it and bring about a more equitable balance of power."[34]

Students of the past had blind trust and respect for school officials, but now school officials have to prove they deserve that respect and trust. Their authoritarian language deprives them of the chance to prove it. Absence of a more encouraging language in our schools is killing education in America. Remember, Peters and Waterman said that in the good companies, a special language that focused on people was present. The same holds true for schools, but educators have not come close to recognizing this unseen enemy in education.

Our young people have been balancing the power, the abused authority used on them, by generating forces to combat it. These forces include slackening efforts in order to control quality pertaining to educational outcomes. Many of our nation's young people still do not graduate from high school. Many dropouts just validate the fact that power used on them made learning so unpleasant that they tried to work around being part of the process.

Students balance the power used on them by withdrawing effort and by controlling the quality of the product they are supposed to produce. No clearer message has been sent to a country attempting to solve a major problem than the message sent by the slackening efforts of students in our schools. Avoiding the research that tells us what is causing this lackadaisical effort is going to catch up with us in the near future.

High-profile, autocratic, traditional teaching is smothering the natural desire to learn in our young people. Once a victim of the autocratic system, a young, growing, vulnerable person will begin to sort out feelings instead of paying attention. This sorting out of feelings is far more important to him than geometry, geography, or genetics is at any particular moment. His sense of belonging may be at stake as well as his self-esteem and security—all basic needs.

If a teacher says, "Sammy, if I have to tell you again to turn around, you will be sent to the office." Sammy will be concentrating on his own feelings and will not be able to concentrate on the assignment. He will be concerned about being somewhat afraid of the teacher's threats because he knows the office does not sound like a safe place to be. He is now off the content of the lesson because he is concentrating on his own emotions.

Millions of these high-profile, power-oriented controls are used daily in the nation's schools. They are a major reason so many students are off task. Teachers, like managers, with their traditional motivational methods, are the reasons the students are off task. Once they are off task, we erroneously make them go to school longer, take more classes, fulfill more requirements, and study harder to make up for the knowledge we helped them lose in the first place.

Since we are supposedly dedicated to education, we could benefit by implanting in the minds of all educators, especially those in the education hierarchy, a good definition of teaching: the ability to inspire learning.

We must also realize that teaching is an instantaneous response profession. Teachers have questions, comments, problems, and requests whizzed by them nearly all day long. They must be better trained to respond not only in an encouraging manner, but also in an instantaneous, intrinsic, and consistently inspirational manner that promotes self-discipline, self-approval, and productivity.

It has been suggested that a revolution is needed in the training of managers, and this holds true for those active in education. Top officials in each field are allowed to interpret the research as they see fit. The result is the usual top-down analysis and recommendations as they fit into the plans to keep the power-based hierarchy intact.

Educators are some of our nation's most important people in helping to develop highly motivated people. Poor development processes in our schools lead to all kinds of problems in the workplace. For this reason teachers, coaches, secretaries, custodians, aides, paraprofessionals, administrators, and others working in our schools must be trained in the special language so they might instill intrinsic motivation into young people. They must be taught to use these concepts daily and consistently. The special language must be heard by students in our classrooms and offices, on our athletic fields, in hallways, lunchrooms and locker rooms. Current autocratic methods of training are perpetuating poor discipline and poor teaching.

Dr. Lewis Losoncy, known worldwide for his books and speeches on encouragement and motivation, sheds light on what happens when our nation's young people get soured on the learning process. He suggests that we ask kindergarten children how they like school, and then ask senior high school students the same question.[35]

Dr. Losoncy asks, "What happens along the way to people to make them lose the naturalness, enthusiasm, and desire for growth?"[35]

He suggests that people develop this more calcified trend as a result of insensitive social relationships. Remember Einstein noted that we strangle the holy curiosity of inquiry. It is likely that we strangle it with insensitive relationships. We strangle it without ever stopping to discover how. We do it with traditional, ingrained remarks that cause resentment and promote friction and a lack of cooperation that impede growth.

The problem with our high-profile comments that cause students to lose their naturalness, enthusiasm, and desire for growth is, according to Carl Rinne, "They are the norm rather than the exception." It is interesting that Rinne noted, "A few teachers in our schools" use low-profile controls.[33] He stated,

> In nearly every United States elementary or secondary school there is at least one teacher who intuitively understands how to control student attention efficiently without interruptions and distractions. Such teachers know that attention to the teacher reduces the time that students pay attention to the lesson, therefore, they design lessons carefully to promote a high level of student attention and then manage the lesson to maintain that attention. Such teachers are typically the best teachers in the school.[33]

The word *intuitively* suggests that good teaching skills are not being taught in teacher training schools, but are somewhat genetic in their source. Have we arrived at the point where we must admit that good teachers are produced through the luck of genetics? What about good managers? If there are only a few teachers in each school who are "intuitively" able to keep students on task, the other teachers must be using top-down, high profile controls. The use of these high-profile techniques is the culprit behind the *A Nation at Risk* report that stated we must keep students on task.

A major problem in education in America is the fact that most teachers believe they are the intuitively blessed, master teachers in a school. Note that managers in business held similar illusions about themselves.

It is sad that members of the hierarchical administrative teams assigned to evaluate teachers have been given little or no training in the low-profile concept. It is difficult for those who have been working in a top-down, power-abusing, hierarchical form of managing people to switch to a system of managing that requires them to understand thoroughly the low-profile approach to motivating people. They must not only be able to recognize the ineffectiveness of the high-profile approach, but also they must be able to teach the low-profile approach.

Without administrators in the schools understanding the low-profile approach and working to install it in their schools, America's educational system will continue to atrophy well into the twenty-first century. It is no different in the business world where businesses will continue to suffer because managers use a high-profile, insulting approach to motivate people toward better productivity.

It is unfortunate that in most school districts, these low-profile people are not viewed as the best teachers. Those who manage our schools still believe in the autocratic control of students. They perpetuate poor teaching and poor discipline. They do so by giving recognition and good performance ratings to the high-profile teachers, often promoting them. The misguided autocratic hierarchy in education was built in the same way as the hierarchies in corporate America.

These high-profile teachers often become part of the management team that makes the schools look good by controlling student behavior. Outside observers of our schools are soon made to believe that learning has to be taking place if everything is so orderly. It is a cosmetic effect because many people associate a strictly ordered environment with one that promotes learning. Spirit killers do not make much noise. Like carbon monoxide gas, they are silent but deadly.

It seems harsh to say that our teachers and administrators, some of the nation's smartest and most dedicated people, are delivering education in an insensitive environment. Perhaps the blow can be softened by reiterating that the American culture overall is not as sensitive and encouraging as most of us would like to believe. It will be a difficult transition for those in education to transform our schools into better places for our young people to learn because most school officials will, as the hierarchy has done in business, cling to the top-down approach.

Motivation and Discipline

Along with the autocratic language used to manage the nation's classrooms, we use poor disciplinary techniques in our schools. Almost invisibly, the autocratic language promotes poor discipline. It promotes a lack of respect for authority we did not see 40 or 50 years ago in schools. It is a major promoter for the slackening of efforts, the disruptive behavior, and the occasional violence in our schools.

We must now assume, based on our knowledge of research into human development and teaching, that autocratically run schools create a very high percentage of their own disciplinary problems. Just as in the business world, the autocratic system of developing people in our schools deprives young people of having their psychological needs met, and that is when the problems arise.

Instead of building up the confidence and self-esteem of students, the system uses embarrassment, fear, and coercion to get youngsters to stay on task and learn. What makes the problem difficult to understand is that these archaic forms of motivation worked in the past.

The changing times make it difficult to understand what is happening in our schools, and we are slow to make adjustments. We need to understand that when a teacher says, "If you are caught cutting class one more time, I will fail you this semester," he or she is not adjusting to the changing times—or to the research. The teacher might say, "You still have a chance at passing this semester, and you can do it. Be here everyday and pass, and you will be proud of what you have done." Often, like the American worker, students have been demotivated and therefore lose enthusiasm to accomplish things.

Alluded to earlier was the fact that legal decisions in the name of justice, not intended for the good development of America or its people, are made daily in this country. In a somewhat predictable decision, the United States Supreme Court, by not hearing cases on the subject, declared that spanking a child in our schools is to be governed by state laws. Some states have recently tried to revive this top-down, high-profile ritual. Socrates seemed to disagree with the Supreme Court when he stated the following:

Violence is a confession of ignorance.

Once again, the hierarchy perpetuated an authoritarian, demeaning, top-down form of motivation. A high court in Italy ruled out spanking of children in that country, but America does not see the need to stop the little things that promote our world-renowned violence.

One community in the Midwest got so desperate to keep students in school that the local police were allowed to ticket them for skipping classes.

When the picture in education eventually becomes clearer to us, we will see that we cannot make laws to enforce learning any more than we can coerce people to work harder. Some schools make their own laws and send the least academic of students to "compulsory" study halls. There is no such thing as "compulsory study." It does not and cannot exist. No human being can be compelled to study. Many students have proven this is true. Terms such as *compulsory study* should begin to tell top-down school management teams that good development has to be influenced and nurtured, not forced.

As education and business in the United States must discover, self-reliance, self-discipline, and self-motivation can be taught to young people. Far too often, when we say things to a young person such as, "You will never make anything out of yourself if you don't study," we do nothing to enhance the possibility of him making something out of himself. Why take chances on someone's development by using discouraging words in relating to them? We must always keep in mind that insensitive social relationships are the ingredients in our society that cause people to lose enthusiasm for life. If we always look for the best in people and convey that to them in encouraging, positive language, we can take pride in our skills to help someone develop.

Much has been written about the vandalism around schools. These crimes are strikes back against the autocratic system. They are usually committed by students who have become victims of the spirit-diminishing, top-down form of development. Once the high-profile controls take hold in a school, the rebellion begins. By rebelling, the students, like workers, send out all kinds of signals that they do not like the way they are being governed. We observe the rebellion daily in our schools, yet we still wonder why students set off fire alarms, throw paint on buildings, break windows, kick in lockers, cut classes, cheat, fight, and generally look at school as a necessary evil.

There is no question that the *A Nation at Risk* report was correct in reporting that we must develop ways to keep our students on task—paying more attention in class and being in class daily during the school year. Our current disciplinary techniques serve to add to the on-task problem. Drop in to any American high school during the day and observe how many students are on the absentee list or in the office each period, and therefore off task.

Many students have been sent to the office by a teacher for being disruptive or uncooperative in class. Others see the school nurse for a multitude of ailments that we cannot deny often originate with discouraging, feelingless remarks. Often, they are just sick of school and the discouraging environment. Other students pick up passes for being tardy or absent. It is fortunate for us that we have many resilient young people who bounce back and, despite the autocratic atmosphere, survive and go on. A school environment, however, should be set up so students do not have to survive it. It should, like the world of work, be motivational, encouraging, and inspirational.

Those students in our schools who take issue with the high-profile, authoritarian form of discipline are usually looked upon as being anti-establishment, rebellious, or just plain troublemakers. Many people look at this rebellion as a lack of respect for authority, and they expect schools to teach students to respect authority. Spirit-killing, authoritarian environments do not respect the psychological needs of students, so they rebel. Then we do not understand their behavior, so we brand it as a lack of respect for authority.

Many students whom we call "dropouts" are really psychologically forced out the door. Their needs are deposited at the door. They cannot handle the insensitivity put upon them. If the education hierarchy continues to make sure our teachers and administrators can improperly use confrontation, praise, questions, power, external motivation, and other spirit killers, our schools will continue to deteriorate. Students will be managed out the door.

In the United States, education and business management typically put off dealing with whatever comes until tomorrow, not realizing that what they do or do not do with people today affects tomorrow twofold. Since both institutions have kept research-proven motivational and disciplinary methods on the back burner, they have significantly altered things they could have accomplished. The organizational structure of our school system is antiquated, and government and educational leaders must begin now to influence radical change for the future. The term *school reform* is popular, but merely lip service for the hierarchy. In business, productivity will not increase until management improves. In education, learning will not improve until teaching improves.

One of the best insights into school discipline and motivation was presented by Dr. Amitai Etzioni, a sociologist and professor at George Washington University in Washington, D.C. Dr. Etzioni believes that the conditions under which students are asked to learn are not the problem. The problem lies in the psychological atmosphere found in most schools. He remarked,

> There is a widespread lack of motivation and ability to apply one's self, defer gratification, to make an effort for later rewards.[36]

Dr. Etzioni noted how threats, sanctions, and penalties are still popular methods to achieve obedience to the school rules. He proclaimed, "It is basically an authoritarian, and suppressive approach . . . Students are forced to learn by rote, to not ask questions and accept elders' dictates." He urged the schools to create an atmosphere where students could "develop their own internal voices of authority" and grow able to "mobilize themselves to the tasks at hand."[36] Dr. Etzioni added,

> Obedience is deceptive: It generates the appearances of an educational environment by imposing order, but underneath it there simmers alienation and rebellion, which hinder the essential internalization of authority. In effect, true education, proper personality development is being undercut.[36]

Is not Dr. Etzioni talking about a force that is present in our schools that prevents self-discipline and self-reliance? Does he not agree that there is widespread demotivation in our schools? Part of what he believes is missing has to be our special language and our ability to rid ourselves of our powerful spirit killers. The problem is, we must inform more people of the cause of the demotivation and start making corrections instead of just dealing with symptoms, before the past neglect ruins our future.

A major cause of widespread slackening efforts in students is, of course, the educational hierarchy making decisions that pump life into the spirit-killing forms of motivation. One of these decisions is to move teachers, who have little idea as to what concepts help promote good discipline and motivation, into administrative positions. These dedicated educators have limited skills as far as helping a teaching staff develop the skills that can promote self-discipline in students. Research has been telling us that the special interpersonal language that motivates all people must become a part of any highly successful teaching staff or management team.

People in teaching are moved up in the hierarchical structure just like in the business world—solely because they are high-profile, rather autocratic, aggressive, and power-oriented in their methods of working with people. This hierarchical arrangement has caused our once-proud educational system to receive much due criticism throughout the world.

In school management today, we now have the untrained evaluating and promoting the untrained.

The famous *Peter Principle,* devised and published by the late Dr. Lawrence Peter, proclaimed that hierarchies keep moving people into positions until they reach their level of incompetence. Now, years after Dr. Peter's book became a best-seller, we see how this theory holds true, not only in education, but business as well.

In education, somewhat as in business, the sad situation is that the hierarchy is able to camouflage its inability to get the best out of people. It is tragic that these educators set examples for young teachers. The older guard, in teaching with autocratic backgrounds, perpetuate the not-so-inspirational atmosphere found in the nation's schools. After we see students wallow in this atmosphere, we ask what happens to our young people as they pass through our educational institutions that causes them to lose their naturalness, enthusiasm, and desire for growth.

No Excuses!

Our current system of education keeps more young people off task than ever before, yet we blame them for not wanting to learn. To assume someone does not want to learn defies the basic nature of man, which is to seek meaning and put life into understandable terms.

Young people learn how not to learn, and we must face up to the fact that our poorly managed schools contribute to that end. Our current spirit-killing methods of motivation thwart learning and are the most devastating elements found in management in education. When it comes to discussing school reform, these elements are the most neglected because they are the least understood.

We have no excuse anymore to not improve our schools. Training can be made available, and through this training, we can stop doing those things that never work. We can put an end to our discouraging communication styles by implementing the special language into all schools. We know that this language is characteristic of good businesses in America, and it must become characteristic of good schools.

Many teachers today say that they already do that when it is suggested they take a look at the special language recommended to improve instruction. Those who undergo intense interpersonal communication scrutiny soon discover that a great many things they normally say to students are demotivational. For a teacher or administrator to deny the value of this type of training is perhaps the greatest cop-out in education today, just as it is a cop-out in business management.

In regard to the training available to help implement the special language, several experts have published material that would be helpful in creating the environment designed to keep students on task. Dr. Thomas Gordon, whose book *L.E.T.—Leader Effectiveness Training* was mentioned in the section on business, also wrote *T.E.T.—Teacher Effectiveness Training.* Dr. Lynette Long wrote *Listening/Responding—Human Relations Training for Teachers.* But these books have not been used to the extent they should to create the proper environment in our businesses and schools. The tools to change education are available, but the willingness of leaders lingers.

There is just no question that we do not have any excuse for failing to implement the special, more encouraging language into our nation's schools. We continue, however, to use the research the wrong way and to treat the symptoms that education is presenting to us. Even a government sponsored Educational Council arrived at the conclusion that the best way to promote learning in schools is to expand the school year to twelve months. This modification would probably increase problems, as the spirit-killing language would be allowed to just go on longer.

One favorite excuse of the hierarchy in education designed to keep the special language at bay and cling to the spirit killers is to claim the new language, as well as the research, has not shown that it makes a difference. There is tremendous support not to change the way we teach and organize schools because, like businesses, these institutions are among our most traditional in the way they operate. Support from each other is one way for those in the hierarchy in education to work around sound research and writings done by numerous experts.

Dr. Long is one who has made it clear that to follow the research in education is important:

> Research has shown that the way in which teachers interact with their students affects both how students feel about themselves and how they achieve in school.[37]

Does not this sound similar to the halo effect, in which managers at Western Electric in 1927 were shown that they would get more productivity out of those under their supervision if they were able to create a sense of caring that would be apparent to those workers? Why has this interaction been so avoided when describing how those who are appointed to supervise should behave? For America to neglect this research, which applies in education and business, has been embarrassing and costly.

Dr. Long writes some profound passages that might lend credence to the idea that spirit-killing forms of communication should be eliminated quickly in our schools. She has a lot to say about empathy: "Empathic teachers do not evaluate a student's feelings but, rather, try to put themselves in the student's place, so that they can better understand the depth of the student's feelings."[40] Note that it was previously shown how managers in business could benefit from learning how to be more empathetic with employees.

The primary goal of the type of training Dr. Long suggests is to provide teachers with skills that can relay to the students the caring and concern the teachers have for them. Most teachers do care about young people or they would not have gone into the profession. Research has been telling us for a long time now that, even though teachers do care, they are not transmitting this caring attitude to their students. Teachers unwittingly create an environment that is far too autocratic to contain a deep level of caring. Teachers and managers who receive training in counseling skills learn to eliminate prejudices, biases, evaluations of behavior, personal values, or frame of references. All of these are things that get in the way when trying to help someone develop. They are, perhaps, the most invisible of our spirit killers. They are difficult to understand in terms of how they get in the way of helping someone. Understanding the special, people-oriented language assists in overcoming these things that can hinder the interaction between teacher and student.

Although we no longer have an excuse not to implement this new language, the use of it will be strange. Change is strange. It takes courage and a deep commitment to understand the psychological needs of people, especially young people. If change came easily, we would change more often to counteract problems in our society.

The first step in making needed communication changes is having teachers and administrators hear themselves say things to students that do not motivate. This can help educators learn what they are saying that is not so inspirational to students. This can best be done by tape recording themselves or taking notes. It will take intensive training with a trained expert for those well-set in their communication patterns to eliminate spirit-killing language and to substitute the more encouraging language.

It is easier to make excuses for our behavior than to make changes in it. This is, essentially, what the hierarchy in education has done for the last several years while education has been under attack in America. The more excuses we make not to reorganize our schools, the more deterioration we will see in the years ahead.

The Vicious Circle

Although nearly invisible, there is a vicious circle in education that helps perpetuate the problems we are encountering in providing true, intrinsic motivation for our young people. An attempt is made here to explain this costly dilemma.

Parents are usually vitally interested in education, and local administrators, in order to keep their jobs, must cooperate with school boards and parents. Teachers are usually willing to serve and try to meet the needs of the students as prescribed by the community officials managing the schools. Herein lies the problem.

In most cases, parents have little or no knowledge of the human development and communication skills that research infers we should implement. As a result, they are limited as far as offering good ideas to the school administration about how their young people should be developed. The parents usually support the old-fashioned, traditional means of whipping someone into shape. Administrators usually agree because they have been raised in similar backgrounds, and their training did nothing to change their views on motivation.

In addition to this parent dilemma, if it is true that only a few teachers in each building intuitively know how to be effective in helping young people learn and develop, why should we believe that many people in the community know the correct way to motivate, teach, and develop people? We know that most parents and teachers do not think of discipline in terms of instilling self-discipline in young people. Even to think it and to have the skill in doing it are, as we have learned, two different things.

Those who have studied the research in education know that the psychological atmosphere in which we ask young people to learn should be revitalized. It is a dilemma we must face that there are just not enough people in a community who recognize the spirit-killing forces that are ruining our schools. A few voices in a community speaking out against the traditional ways of doing things in education are just not going to be enough to stop the trend toward mediocrity.

The inability to see problems in the traditional approach in education helps the vicious circle continue because parents reinforce the autocratic style. Of course, administrators agree and do so for two basic reasons. The reasons are devastating to our current system of management in education.

The first reason is that, though no fault of their own, most administrators have not had the intensive training they need to implement these skills. Many administrators are in the twilight of their careers, are very traditional, and do not wish to study anymore. Those who have had minimal training in the special language do not recognize it as the major ingredient that the research and educational experts tell us it is. In the schools these administrators manage, a change in motivational style through improved communication becomes a fad, touched upon briefly during teachers' institutes, and then forgotten.

The second reason is, any administrator who makes a big push to implement a more encouraging, sensitive atmosphere in a school will run into terrific opposition. The majority of parents, teachers, and administrators will see this new approach as being too easy on kids or destructive to the normal way schools are managed. Some will say, "We cannot coddle kids and also toughen them up for the outside world." The educational hierarchy has so many clever built-in excuses to prolong the traditional way, it will be extremely difficult to implement a special language in many schools. The fact is, we can toughen up kids for the outside world by making them confident in themselves and giving them the spirit they will need to deal with tough situations the world presents to them.

Young people who grow into adulthood who have had their self-esteem ripped apart and their spirits broken by spirit-killing remarks by well-meaning adults, are the people who often strike back at a society.

Traditionalists in education will say that the schools will look disorganized, that students will get out of control, and good old-fashioned discipline must be the standard. School administrators, like managers in business, figure that if they do not go along with the traditional, top-down movement, they could be looking for a job. They soon acquiesce for their own security, and we know this security is a basic need. The top-down management style is so well entrenched in education that the infection spreads itself throughout a community. Once it has its strangle hold on enough influential people, it can threaten the jobs and the security of those who attempt to change it. It is not well known to the general public, but courageous educators who have tried to make changes in the top-down management and teaching styles in our schools have either been run out of those schools or are avoided like a nest of irritated bees.

The prevailing attitude in most communities among parents, teachers, and administrators keeps the schools traditional, but not as effective as they could be. It is a vicious circle or, at least, a stubborn hierarchy made up of community members who are probably functioning in an hierarchy themselves. It is going to be a difficult cycle to break, but it will have to be broken sometime in the twenty-first century.

The vicious circle has tentacles that reach to the top in a community—to school board members, who are usually our rather traditional, autocratic, old-school type of people who resist any kind of change that they think might make their schools look disorderly. When it is suggested by someone that a school is too tight, most board members in America today respond with bewilderment, convinced that the tighter, the better.

"What was good enough for us is good enough for our children," proclaim many school board members throughout America. Who can blame school board members for wanting orderly schools? But sound educators know that we mistake an obedient, forced environment for one in which real learning is taking place. Spirit killers run rampant in these orderly schools and the vicious circle keeps on rolling.

We can see now that our educational institutions are largely managed by people who have training in a multitude of things—except human development, motivation, interpersonal communication, learning theories, personality theories, educational psychology, and discipline. These are the ingredients that would allow people to work together to implement new, more motivational programs that would eventually get a better effort out of our young people.

School board members do not have much in common regarding educational background and school management, except one characteristic—they went to school! Research shows that is not very strong training. School board members, many of whom are in a high level of management in the business world, are often products of autocratic homes that relied on external means of motivation and strict obedience demanded by autocratic parents. (This is a major factor in how the top-down approach to managing people is transferred from business to education.) Years ago, when respect for authority went unquestioned, this form of development worked. In today's America, those who are chosen to lead our schools must realize that times have changed, and young people, like American workers, cry out for more democratic, caring procedures.

Many parents (who might be school board members) take away the stereo, the car, the headphones, or the weekend privileges to externally motivate their young people or to punish them. One student said, "My folks are in a real bind. They have taken so much away from me, they don't have anything left to take."

From school boards on down, we are so entrenched in external motivation, order, obedience, and high-profile forms of motivation that we lose sight of the fact that all of this is not instilling self-discipline and keeping students on task. It is doing the opposite, and that is one reason the schools are catching so much heat from so many different sources. We spend so much time demanding order that we cannot see we are developing disorderliness in our young people.

School board members are some of the most conscientious, dedicated, hard-working, intelligent people in our country. Nevertheless, school boards throughout America must now consider that their leadership actually contributes to our demise, our being at risk. Education is the only institution in America that is managed and controlled by people who have little or no training in its most important mission—human development.

To demonstrate how the hierarchy perpetuates the autocratic forces now so devastating our schools, consider the following as a typical example of what goes on in our schools.

A top administrator in a large Chicago suburban district had completed some training pertaining to how to keep students on task. She was going over the new motivational method with a group of teachers. The administrator said, "We must keep students on task. If a student is not working on an assignment and is somewhat out of order, the teacher should not embarrass the student by singling him out, but stand beside the student. It is very difficult to misbehave when the teacher is breathing just above you."

The vicious circle continues because the administrator, unwittingly, keeps the traditional, high-profile form of control intact. She does so by encouraging teachers to stand by a student and obviously strike fear into that misbehaving student by breathing just above him. The administrator has simply replaced embarrassment with fear. This example shows how the "on task" research has been misinterpreted and how the autocratic system maintains its stranglehold.

Remember that fear is the primary source of motivation in the business world. The above example shows that same source is used in education.

Today's business management tries to frighten people into working harder, and such motivation has been transferred into education, where we try to frighten students into learning more.

Instead of using the fear tactic in the example above, the teacher should have said something like, "Everyone should stay on task and do your best with this assignment." This rules out embarrassment and fear, and allows the misbehaving student to make his own decision about completing the assignment. We need to understand that we cannot coerce people into learning because then it becomes learning that will not last.

The majority of those interested in education would sanction the type of control explained by the administrator in the above example. If she were being given a performance review, chances are she would be rated highly as standards go in education today. None of the teachers present questioned the method. Students do not, in the long run, respond to fear any better than employees, but many teachers fight to keep fear as a form of control because they believe it makes their jobs easier. Since most officials in the school and community have autocratic backgrounds, the teachers can gain support, a form of security, from their bosses and parents.

Use of fear in managing our schools is almost like an invisibly agreed-to conspiracy. To be strict in a nation that seems to be developing more and more people who lack self-discipline is the right approach, as far as traditionalists are concerned. Few understand that the use of fear and other spirit killers in our institutions is the cause of the lack of self-discipline in people. Self-discipline is nurtured not commanded, influenced not pressured, stimulated not demanded. Leadership in most organizations does not understand that such stimulation may take a little longer than using fear, power, embarrassment, and all of our other spirit killers.

In sanctioning the vicious circle, many administrators think that if they become anymore democratic, they will lose control; so the power game goes on. They do not realize that they have already set into motion those ingredients in a school that promote poor self-discipline by encouraging top-down governing and instruction.

Most communities take great pride in their schools and how they are managed. Every principal, superintendent, and board member believes that the research is pointing a finger at other schools. This attitude is part of the hierarchical dilemma that prevents the change our schools are going to need sometime in the twenty-first century. The attitude is just part of the vicious circle. As in business, leaders in education can stop the downward trend in motivation and learning by being realistic about what the research reveals.

The Vicious Circle in Government Affects Education

Federal and state governments are part of the vicious circle that is swiftly rolling over education. The *A Nation at Risk* report, compiled by the federal government, told education leaders what was wrong with education, but not what could be done about it. That is working against education now that the "on task" portion of the report was left up to interpretation by those who control the direction of education in each state. Interpretations were made by the education hierarchy, and these interpretations trickled down through state and local governments. Since the government holds the purse strings, many local administrators scurried to implement programs that create an illusion something is being done to keep students on task.

Education administrators are perhaps the best at creating illusions to make their institutions look good.

We have seen one program example where teachers were asked to control a student by standing by and breathing just above the student. Government officials evaluating such programs mistakenly believe that good order brought about by such desperate techniques promotes good discipline. The real meaning of the research lies buried as leaders in education implement programs, thinking that good order in the schools promotes students being on task. A ten-year follow-up of the *A Nation at Risk* report revealed that not much had been accomplished in improving education, and nothing was mentioned about a special language being implemented to help keep students on task. Such results should not be surprising.

In managing education, we cannot be satisfied with creating order and just getting young people to class. We have for too long associated attendance with learning. Some states appropriate money based on ADA, average daily attendance. We are only going to be able to justify our educational management efforts when more people can read, write, and compute well enough to stay off welfare and support families. This means that self-discipline must be instilled into more of the nation's young people so they will be able to make better decisions and seek more meaning in their lives. If they discipline themselves and learn, meaning will come to them.

In addressing the issue of control and self-discipline in the schools, Dr. Amitai Etzioni mentioned that this is still a confusing issue for government. He noted that as far back as President Reagan's administration, government favored "greater use of police departments to restore law and order in the schools." The President used the term *old-fashioned discipline*. Dr. Etzioni noted the remarks of President Reagan and his "various spokesmen" who talked about "millions of incidents of physical attacks on pupils and thousands of threatened or abused teachers." Dr. Etzioni noted that "discipline as obedience" appealed to Reagan and, as has been explained, this appeal for more obedience in schools is a popular way for politicians and educational leaders to address the deterioration in education as we enter the twenty-first century.

Dr. Etzioni wrote that violence of the type where police have to be called to a school is not rampant and "is not at the root of what troubles most of them." He reflected on President Reagan's views of discipline and suggested they were outdated and would not benefit the schools. He commented that President Reagan was told that "calling the police into the schools cost little," and "politically, the call for strict discipline is a winner."[36]

Dr. Etzioni held a different, more accurate view of how to bring about good discipline in our schools. He seemed to be in tune with the research when he wrote,

---

Our future, however, requires open, adaptive, creative persons; individuals able to develop new technologies and new techniques not assembly-line automations but professionals, computer programmers, knowledge engineers and others who can follow their own lights without slackening on the job.[36]

It is clear that President Reagan and other politicians who have followed him figured that if students are not learning at a rate that could keep America's future from being at risk, the schools will have to implement "controls" to get "obedience" that would get more out of students. The politicians wrongly convey that learning can be forced and that creating strict order is the key.

What would the police departments do to increase learning? Placing armed policemen with walkie-talkies and trained German shepherds in the hallways of schools may produce a more subdued atmosphere. (Students might get in the classrooms quicker!) If the teachers and administrators continue to use the spirit-killing language that sets off the violence, the police and their dogs will not be able to prevent the violence; they can only deal with it after the fact.

It is clear that federal authorities interpreted the research in such a way that underachievement in our students was given prolonged life. When our leaders in state government and our local school superintendents, board members, and other officials mistakenly make such appraisals, how can we make any progress in correcting the ills in education?

Our schools, thanks to misguided government intervention and the hierarchical, top-down management systems, have built up a blind trust. The general public believes the schools are getting worse, but it also believes in the management hierarchy when school reforms and school accountability programs are announced. It is as though we think the next innovation will work. We have blind faith in our institutions when we should be questioning to the smallest detail what effect the management in these institutions has on us and the future of our country.

It should be clear that educating and motivating our young people as well as management in our schools has become political. The government participates in the vicious circle because politicians see old-fashioned methods of motivation as politically correct. They jump on the bandwagon with those who believe old-fashioned discipline is the answer to improve learning. They do so because it is clear that more voters believe in this style. It is alarming that so many politicians back programs that perpetuate outdated programs that are intended to get a better effort out of students. It is alarming because they do not read the research. They become part of an elitist hierarchy that contributes to educational problems instead of solving them.

The hierarchy in education correctly passed on some information to teachers. Research was explicit in showing that students needed to be kept on task and that teachers should have high expectations of them. We now know, through research, that if a teacher somehow conveys to a student that he or she is not capable of a strong performance, the student will perform to those low expectations. If high expectations are present, there is a good chance the student will perform well. Of course, our hidden spirit killers help relay low expectation to students.

As usual, no training was provided as to how to instill these high expectations in students. It was incorrectly assumed that more homework and tougher assignments were in order because this would show high expectations. It was not considered that our spirit-killing language could invisibly transmit low expectations and destroy attempts to implement this part of the research.

Educators, like corporate managers, will have to consider that high expectations cannot be externally transmitted. The traditional methods of teaching often externally transmit to young people that they are not capable. These methods project the attitude that the teacher does not have the time to listen to feelings, and to deny feelings is to transmit a non-caring atmosphere. By doing this, teachers constantly transmit to students that they do not care about their development, and therefore students do not develop as they should. By neglecting research, education has fulfilled a prophecy that some experts predicted for it—poorly managed schools.

It is fortunate for us that the spirit of many students to seek meaning, to strive, to learn, and seek recognition is not dead. It has only been wounded by the discouraging managing and instructional systems in our schools. There is time, before we get too far into the twenty-first century, to revive the spirit in many school systems. We need to develop students so more of them want to learn because they have high expectations of themselves and want to expand their horizons. Young people will not produce more because we want them to; they will do it because it has been instilled in them that it is best for them.

Law and Order, or Orderliness and Self-Discipline?

A Nation at Risk had a tremendous effect on top leaders. As pointed out, President Reagan and his aides misinterpreted the research. He gave several key speeches that are still having an effect on teaching and administering as we head into the twenty-first century. His views, largely authoritarian, condoned a law-and-order atmosphere in schools and also hinted that learning could be forced into students. Following are excerpts from a speech he made to the National Association of Secondary School Principals, a group that later fell into line in regard to the misinterpreted research,

> We cannot allow our children to continue falling behind. Instead, we must insist that all American students master the basics, math, science, history, reading and writing that have always formed the core of our civilization. What is needed, is for children to do more work and better work, and that includes homework. No learning can take place without good order in the classrooms and that means restoring good old-fashioned discipline. In too many classrooms, teachers lack authority to make students take tests, hand in homework or even quiet down in class.[38]

President Reagan acknowledged that our children "continue to fall behind." It is unfortunate that his speech gave the nation's principals encouragement to become more authoritarian while denying the research. He suggested that we can inject knowledge into young people whether they want it or not. Such an attitude persisted throughout the Bush presidency, and President Clinton has done little to correct the situation.

Note that President Reagan stated some things about learning that are diametrically opposite to those things expert writers in management and education have been telling us. He used such phrases as, "We must insist," and "do more homework" and "restore old-fashioned discipline." He remarked that "teachers lack authority to make students take tests," and he said we must have "good order." He conveyed to the school principals a law-and-order, get tougher stance that is typical of autocratic, top-down management. It is a cop-out guaranteed to keep education on hold.

What does old-fashioned discipline mean? Are we to promote pulling ears, pinching, shaking, thumping heads, rapping knuckles, pulling hair, and spanking? Detentions are still found in most schools in America. They are often punishment for not making a good effort to learn.

It is clear that force and fear, two spirit killers, were recommended by President Reagan to improve education. It is clear as Caribbean waters that the top-down style of managing our schools is politically sanctioned, and this creates a stranglehold on American education.

After the *A Nation at Risk* report came out, the educational hierarchy helped spread the impression that more order was needed in schools. This trickled down to the local levels, and this is the reason the law-and-order approach is solidly entrenched today. There is a difference in people being in order as compared to being orderly. The well-respected Rudolph Dreikurs, who wrote about educational problems, said about this important, misunderstood topic:

> It would be more meaningful if we could substitute the word "orderly" for the word "order." Order usually means rigidity. If an individual is to become a useful person, he must adapt himself to some orderly pattern of living, learn to think and act in line with social regulations, adjust to his environment, and develop a sense of responsibility. Individuals cannot live with other persons unless they are guided by certain rules and regulations necessary for happy, peaceful living. It is this process that we call discipline.[39]

Dreikurs goes on to point out that "freedom and order are mutually exclusive" and "order means doing as your told, and there is no freedom of self-determination." He suggests that freedom and order go hand-in-hand. People in any society cannot do whatever they want when their behavior imposes on the freedoms of others. Many of our young people rebel against social regulations, such as the ones in schools, because they see them as being too rigid for their personal development. Remember, people often do things contrary to their belief about those things. Such behavior becomes a subconscious reaction to counter power being used on them. This explains why young people withhold efforts in schools and strike out against authoritarian leadership.

Students are merely exhibiting the same type of behavior as workers in those companies that adhere to top-down management styles. If they do not have any input into those decisions that have an effect on their well-being, the workers look at management as not being worker and family friendly. Students see those who manage our schools as rigid and unbending, as people who want them to do exactly as they are told with little regard to how students feel about the demands. Schools, like businesses, would have a better chance to catch up to the research, so to speak, if they would involve students (and teachers) in more decisions about how the schools are to be managed. Self-discipline, then, would be easier to instill because it is known that people are more likely to abide by rules and regulations they help form.

Dreikurs alluded to the fact that "imposed order is rejected." Nevertheless, our nation's leaders are clearly urging us to implement a law-and-order environment even though this works against the idea that we have to nurture self-discipline in students. We cannot "make students take tests" or "hand in home work"; nor can we "insist" that they master the basics. We cannot make anybody do anything as intrinsic as learning.

Getting the best out of people and helping them develop into physically and mentally healthy, contributing members of society is often frustrating. This frustration is seen in the likes of President Reagan's speech and his law-and-order, coercive form of instruction. It is also seen in parents' trying to develop young people properly. One father became so frustrated with his daughter's anorexia that he tried to force a sandwich down her throat. Such is the thinking of those who believe they can overcome the growing problems of youth by authoritarian means.

Why, after all of the research studies, do we continue to believe that we can impose order and self-discipline? The more order we impose, the less orderliness we are going to get. Why cannot we see that learning in our young people suffers when we use autocratic methods to motivate them, that the methods cause the resentment, discouragement, anger, and fear that diminishes their efforts? Those methods cause young people to be intimidated, ignored, feel powerless, ridiculed, underrated, demoralized, and vulnerable.

It is little wonder that students with these feelings do crazy things that keep administrators hopping to put out brush fires in our schools. Imposed order causes tension; orderliness fostered by self-reliance does not.

Some power, some authority must be present in any organization because total freedom for those who cannot yet handle such freedom can lead to upheaval that could destroy the organization and its mission. The buck has to stop somewhere. Behavior that is antisocial and does not promote social connectiveness should not be tolerated. There must be a final voice if for no other reason than to show those being antisocial to others that to be socially connected for the good of each other is what democracy is all about.

It is just a simple fact that disruption of any kind will occur more frequently in organizations where leaders impose order. Our spirit killers cannot survive in organizations built on orderliness, encouragement, social connectiveness, and trust, but they can have a feast in those where order resembles a mini-dictatorship.

Unless training is implemented on a national level, the current fear of disorder overwhelming our schools will continue to cause school officials to run a tight ship in hope that their school is not singled out as one being out of control. If the schools can display an environment of imposed order that leads to student obedience, reasonable test scores, and good facilities, it has a good chance of being recognized by the government as one achieving excellence in education. Such recognition is one of our greatest cop-outs in an attempt to develop our young people for future challenges.

Anything that gives the impression that learning can be forced should be removed from any educational system. This would include eliminating detentions for students who are not making a good effort to learn because punishment for not learning is similar to giving rewards to those who excel. We must get to the point where we understand that learning and knowledge are the ingredients that will move our country ahead, and neither are best promoted by external means.

Rather than the traditional, autocratic, externally based system, we need to learn how to teach so that it is something that youngsters will not want to stay away from. We need to organize our schools so they promote good human development aided by social connectiveness. Education has joined the ranks of the business world, where it has forgotten how we are all socially connected. Going to work and going to school should become much more enjoyable in America.

Teacher Training and School Accountability

The research in education tells us that we will ultimately have to change the behavior of our teachers just as we will have to change the behavior of managers in business. In today's American educational system, it is unfortunate that administrative teams seldom try to change the behavior of the teacher, at least in terms of the research. Students are always to blame for disruptions in learning. The top-down architects present an illusion, as in most hierarchies, that things are under control by constantly disciplining students.

In American education, the hierarchy is not recognizing that if learning is to get better, so must teaching. Even when the hierarchy in education finally does agree, probably sometime well into the twenty-first century, our enemy within will be extended because it will attempt to make changes in teaching as hierarchies usually do—with the use of power, threats, fear, and intimidation. It follows that those who see change coming in education fear that our next big mistake will be that we attempt to change the behavior of our teachers by using these hopeless, power-based, external methods.

Teachers will not change their behavior and become less autocratic unless it is evident that the powers above them have become less autocratic. To set up this type of change needed in education will take more cooperation between teachers, administrators, and government officials than ever seen before. In the distant future, administrators will be told that we have to change the way we teach, and it will become necessary to teach the teachers how to make these changes.

Few of us can imagine now how our top-down-oriented school administrators are going to teach, or at least nurture, a lower-profile, special-language-enriched teaching staff that can instill orderliness and, thus, learning in students. Teachers cannot be taught to give up power over students by administrators who have not given up their power over teachers. Improved training of our teachers will have to be influenced by administration, just as good learning by students is influenced by teachers.

Unfortunate for education in the twenty-first century is the fact that it is so traditional that there will be those who will try to find holes in the research and set teacher training and school management so far back that education might not ever recover. These traditionalists fit into the category of those spoken of by John Kenneth Galbraith,

> *Faced with having to change our views or prove that there is no need to do so, most of us get busy on the proof.*

Traditional education is so well-accepted that those who believe in it do not have to "get busy on the proof" because they know that proving something invisible, such as learning being intrinsic, is almost impossible for those who claim change is needed.

It should not be surprising that some evidence exists that says external, top-down management for creating better teachers is upon us. Merit pay is a popular external device used to stimulate teachers to coax more out of students. Merit pay is no different in terms of motivation than taking the stereo away from a student or paying for grades. This external motivation cannot be maintained long enough because it loses its value when compared to the motivation that comes from within an individual who wants to become a better teacher. Merit pay has been tried in many school districts, and it fails because it becomes political. Management in education, as things currently stand, is frustrated with the teacher evaluation process, and rightfully so because research is being neglected that could make this process so much easier and more effective.

To guarantee accountability and excellence in our schools, a national plan will have to be developed to convince, influence, and encourage teachers and all others who work in our schools to be retrained. The training would consist primarily of teaching teachers the special language we now know is so important. It would also teach teachers how to say and do things that eliminate external motivation and create an environment that fosters internal motivation. It would show teachers how many discipline problems are caused by the way they relate to students. They would understand that if they give young people a wall to bounce their ball against, they will bounce it.

Once we take away the high-profile form of teaching that research reveals is being used, the youngsters will not have any wall to bounce the system up against. Accountability in the schools of the future will have to be based on almost totally changed methods of observing and evaluating those schools. The only way for anyone to get a good feel for the type of management that promotes orderliness, not strict order, is to be in the school for a long period of time. Schools are currently evaluated over very short periods of time. This will have to change in order to evaluate every school worker in terms of how each relates to students and administers discipline. The same standards would have to apply to administrators.

Only government, whether it be state, federal, or local, can provide the impetus and the money for true school reform in a country that seems to be spending less and less on human development. Many schools spend more money on lunchroom supervision than on staff development. In the top-down management of our schools, staff development has been something that needs to be presented once in a while to maintain the illusion that efforts are made for improvement. Staff development will need to become an ongoing program for many years to come if we are going to overcome the tragic underdevelopment of our youth that is beginning to have a deleterious effect on our country.

Teachers in the future will have to be evaluated in terms of their human developmental skills as well as their knowledge of their subject matter. Performance evaluations would not be punitive, but instead approached only in terms of how well a teacher transmitted both subject matter and human development intangibles through the encouraging special language.

Human technology is so advanced that teachers can now be evaluated in terms of how well they respond to students who confront them or who just talk with them during the school day. They can be taught whether or not they may have sparked the confrontation, and hostile confrontations do take place daily in our schools. Without going into a detailed explanation of a research-based training system, it is possible to measure whether or not anything a teacher says to a student is helpful or hurtful. This is great progress in terms of eliminating our spirit killers, but such programs are not known to be used in any school in the United States.

We are approaching the day when teachers will be monitored by video cameras or tape recorders. The autocratic language, present in all of us, can then be picked out and, with practice, a lower-profile teacher will emerge. Eventually a low-profile school will emerge.

Evaluating the teaching process has always been a complex process, to be sure. They have been a long time coming, but we are discovering ways to be more specific about evaluating teaching skills. In the past, few of our elementary or secondary school teachers spent much time learning how to relate to students. Meetings were held on how to teach math concepts, do a science experiment, control hall passes, or put together a good bulletin board. A great deal of time has been spent on how to motivate students externally.

Typical evaluations of classroom management have included such things as:

- How well did the teacher maintain order?
- Was there eye contact with students?
- Did the teacher move around the room?
- Was the discussion stimulating?

- Were all students included?
- Were lesson plans available?

The general public may not be aware that administrators usually require these plans because they help to create the illusion that good teaching is going on. Lesson plans are something concrete that can be shown to anyone who doubts that the top-down system is working.

Shying away from the critical elements that make for good teaching, administrators evaluating teachers today look for the use of audiovisuals or field trips. Did the teacher use the right colored chalk? Did the teacher use every minute of class time to keep students on task? These classroom procedures are important, but the system fails when high-profile techniques are encouraged. It fails when power is used on students, and those doing the evaluation cannot recognize that it is a detriment to the learning process. Of course, most teachers are going to be on their best behavior while being evaluated, and they will eliminate some of the high-profile techniques. The enemy within our schools is given further life when the spirit-killing language is used and the evaluator does nothing to help the teacher learn how the language is demotivational.

If polled, teachers probably would tell us that evaluations are unavoidable, often rather meaningless, and are usually used to show them how to control students or make the school look good. It is sad that we now have the untrained evaluating the untrained because we have become lost in the control, order, high-profile, obedience-oriented, authoritarian attempts to make the schools look good instead of being good. Current evaluation systems in education promote the autocratic system because they do little to change it. Education is in an either/or situation. Either educators begin to implement the special language, or education will continue to stagnate.

When President Reagan said, "We cannot allow our children to continue to fall behind," he admitted that statistics show we might be at risk in the way we are educating our young people. We cannot wait very long into the future to recognize that our teacher training institutions are contributing their fair share in promoting the high-profile, authoritarian approach to motivating the nation's young people. They do not emphasize the importance of the day-to-day, instantaneous interaction that teachers have with students. Teaching young teachers how to overcome the traditional, authoritarian forms of speaking that most have had unwittingly instilled in them by an autocratic coach, teacher, parent, or employer, is not done in most colleges that train teachers.

It is regrettable that even those young teachers who do come from sound training programs will be chewed up by the autocratic system faster than Tom Turkey on Thanksgiving. In order to perpetuate the hierarchy, administrators often mention that it can be dangerous for beginning teachers to try to use low-profile skills because "the kids will run over them." This is, of course, one of the best cop-outs built into the educational hierarchy. So many cop-outs and excuses are used to not implement research-based programs that it is probable education will have to get much worse before undergoing change that will be essential in the twenty-first century.

Student teaching, or practice teaching as it is sometimes called, con-tributes greatly to the chaos in education. Students at universities who are ready to do student teaching are placed in a school to work with a mentor or "practice teacher" to help make the transition from teacher preparation to a teaching position. More often than not, the autocratic, spirit-reducing system is given yet another continuance because the administrative-assigned mentor is from the school of old-fashioned discipline and teaching, and has never heard of the well-researched encouraging language.

The aspiring young teacher is baptized into the educational hierarchical scheme of things, learning high-profile techniques and subtle ways to instill fear in and embarrass young people so the teacher does not have to worry about control problems and is free to teach. Never in the history of a country has such a well-oiled, synchronized, but invisible machine plowed under such a vital component to its well-being.

Students in practice teaching are usually assigned to the highest-profile teachers because these teachers are the ones who continue to breathe life into the hierarchy. Administrators also want to give the impression that the build-ing is under strict control. If it is under control, then learning must be taking place. That is the game the hierarchy in education is playing . . . and losing.

Experienced teachers who become practice teachers usually do not under-stand that it is best to work with students so they might develop self-control and self-approval. Once all students understand the concept of developing self-approval, the best form of control has been established. Of course, this would be utopia, but we can do much better than we are doing. Mentors in the teaching profession often do the exact opposite. They teach in the authoritar-ian way that turns youngsters off; then it is a struggle to turn them back on. Instead of put-downs in our schools, we need put-ups. Supervising teachers experienced in the special language could be relaying this message to young, incoming teachers so we might be able to develop more low-profile teachers and, eventually, low-profile schools.

Let us look at one more example, just as a reminder, of how the special language could be taught to a student teacher, but is overlooked by a supervising teacher. Assume that before the start of a class, which the student teacher is observing, a student says to the experienced teacher, "Can I skip the film today and read? I have to finish my book report by tomorrow. I have not had the time since my English teacher gave me the assignment two days ago."

The teacher says, "I doubt if any teacher here would give you that much to do in such a short time. It does not sound like you planned too well. I can't allow you to miss the film."

When the teacher said, "I doubt" and "you didn't plan too well," he was being critical as well as evaluating the student's behavior. He was judging him and possibly making an assumption. All of these remarks are potential spirit killers. They can set off resentment that stalls learning.

Most important, the supervising teacher was showing the aspiring teacher a classic example of how feelings are left out of our schools and how spirits are diminished. The student was feeling anxious, swamped, overwhelmed, rushed, pressed, or something close to these feelings. The teacher, like a good manager, could have been more empathetic to the student and said something like, "It does sound like you are anxious about your report. I can tell you are pressed, but it is very important that all members of our class see the film this period."

The teacher's response does not solve the student's problem, but it does not add to it. This approach has a much better chance of avoiding conflict and keeping the student on task . . . and the relationship stays in good standing. The student's feelings are not bruised, and he is not attacked with spirit-killing words or phrases.

In this example, the student's request was not reasonable, but the teacher could have responded in a less blaming way, and responded to the feeling, not the event. Research tells us it is important to accept and acknowledge feelings, and good teachers and good managers know how to do this. It is important for experienced teachers to pass concepts like this on to young aspiring teachers, but it is not being done often enough.

We know that Dr. Gordon wrote about and believed that the mystery has been taken out of what constitutes good leadership qualities. These qualities apply to good managers in the business world as well as to good teachers. We need a more systematic approach in both fields to make certain these good qualities are implemented to help eradicate the spirit-killing environments found in them.

President Roosevelt tried to tell us over fifty years ago that we must culti-vate the science of human relationships. How far have we come in accom-plishing this cultivation when the Chicago city schools have to spend money to place metal detectors at the doors of the schools so students do not bring in guns and knives? It is predictable that school authorities claim that such at-titudes originate in the streets and have little to do with the attitudes devel-oped in the schools. We must understand that the spirit killers do not have any boundaries. Young people are motivated or demotivated to develop inner voices of self-discipline wherever they go.

Institutions cannot be totally blamed for the misbehavior of people, but it is erroneous to believe that the autocratic environments found in them do not contribute significantly to antisocial behavior.

For any school to claim that feelings of discouragement are not picked up by young people in these traditional institutions is to add copping out to the hierarchy. Explosive feelings such as resentment, apprehension, alienation, ex-clusion, and loneliness carry over from the schools into the streets of our cities. The feelings are also expressed by students in various ways when they attend the schools that have rejected the research and maintained the demo-tivating authoritarian approach to teaching. Spirit-killing remarks can be more harmful than weapons. Note that we have yet to put spirit-killing detec-tors at the doors of any school.

It seems as though only a few leaders can connect the idea that intimacy lacking in our institutions causes problems for the entire country. Business complains that high schools need to be reorganized to ready people for the work force. Business officials do not seem to understand that the top-down form of managing has been transplanted into the school systems and causes human development problems blamed entirely on the schools. This is just an-other one of our vicious circles that keeps the authoritarian system alive.

The absence of a system that could help put intimacy into our workplaces and schools causes suicide, alcohol and drug addictions, unwanted pregnan-cies, eating disorders, mental problems, behavioral disorders, thievery, apathy, violence, stress, and medical problems. It is for these reasons that we must change the way we approach motivation in today's America.

A primary obstacle to overcome, whether it be in education or business, is the lack of proper training required of aspiring leaders. The training would assist them in zeroing in on their own top-down style of communicating which affects their ability to motivate others. This training would promote the intimacy, social connectiveness, and harmony so much needed in all of our institutions. We could begin to restructure the powerful management pyramids.

Following is a list of suggestions that can help anyone change an autocratic attitude into a democratic attitude. It is unfortunate that such suggestions have been around for a long, long time, but they have been ignored by management in both education and business. Most of the items on the autocratic side of the listing are used too frequently in America's institutions.

Autocratic	Democratic
Boss	Leader
Sharp voice	Friendly voice
Command	Invitation
Power	Influence
Pressure	Stimulation
Demands cooperation	Wins cooperation
I tell you what you should do	I tell what I would like to do
Imposes ideas	Sells ideas
Dominates	Guides
Criticizes	Encourages
Finding fault	Acknowledges achievement
Punishes	Helps
I tell you	Discusses
I decide, you obey	I suggest and help you to
Has sole responsibility of group	Share responsibility of team[39]

> Our failure to expertly monitor education in terms of what goes on in the interaction between students and all school personnel has been a major part of the downfall of education in America.

Every school, and every institution for that matter, should strive hard to implement the democratic side of the above listing. Rest assured that it will take a change in attitude and in language to make the transition from an autocratic environment to a democratic one. It will also take a lot of pain, a lot of time, and intricate negotiations between management and employees.

In attempting to make changes, there will be encounters with those who want to maintain autocratic environments because it is easier for them. They mistakenly believe such environments get the best efforts out of people. On the democratic side, there will be those who understand what the research is saying, and they will no longer want to wallow in mediocrity, or even worse, total decay.

Making the schools democratic in tone will help to eliminate many of the cop-outs the hierarchy cleverly builds into the system. One such cop-out that is currently kicked around in education is the idea that many teachers do not know their subject matter. This notion has caused many to say we must work to get brighter people to go into education. There is no evidence that teachers who obtain better grades in college will be the best teachers. Knowing the subject matter is one thing; transmitting the knowledge is still another. As we now know, the best teachers are those who can relate to their students, motivate them, and keep them on task.

Excuses for the failure of education are plentiful, but the teacher–student relationship is the thing that will have to be concentrated on if we are to have any chance to improve education in the future.

Effort put anywhere else can be chalked up to the hierarchy's ability to keep the vicious circle rolling on; then the cop-outs revitalize themselves. Those interested in education can, with a dedicated effort, help formulate a systematic approach to teaching young people that will not feel systematic after it is implemented properly. Some difficult questions must first be answered:

- How can teacher-training institutions be influenced to teach research-based skills and democratic attitudes?
- How can we improve practice teaching to include these skills and change attitudes?
- How can we help school administrators understand the new human relations skills and gain the expertise needed to help teachers implement these skills?
- How can we help teachers, who are now teaching and will be well into the twenty-first century, revise some long-held autocratic attitudes and change their methods of teaching?

- How do we convince people in a community, especially school board members who have not had the training, that these new methods are sound?
- How do we help parents understand and accept these new, research-based programs that lead to more democratic schools?
- How can we monitor schools to ensure that a more positive tone prevails once the training becomes universal?

The state of Indiana in House Bill 1105 at least made an attempt to include communication skills as part of an exam for teachers seeking licensing. It is doubtful that such a bill would include eliminating the spirit-killing form of language currently used in top-down managed schools, but it is a start. Exams for the language will not suffice. Monitoring the exchanges in a classroom between the teacher and the students is what is needed. In fact, words spoken throughout the school by everyone associated with it will have to be under scrutiny until everyone is comfortable with the changes. The systematic approach must be set up so when elementary students enter junior high schools, the language spoken to motivate them is consistent with the language they have been hearing in their previous schools. The same systemwide approach would have to prevail for junior high students entering high schools.

There is a well-known phrase in America that sums up a national attitude about teaching: Those who can't, teach. This phrase sums up the idea that if an individual cannot do anything else, he should try teaching because anyone can do it. If anyone can do it, why do we read so many articles and see so many television programs that tell us that teaching and education are in such disarray? It takes a lot of study, observation, and concentration on a daily basis to become a good teacher. We need better managed schools and better teachers to prepare us for the twenty-first century. Neglecting the research will only cause a delay in the needed changes.

We are not getting the best out of our young people, just as we are not getting the best out of our workforce. We cannot allow the difficulty of changing school management to prevent us from making education effective. We must make the traditional, ineffective forces that are destroying education obsolete.

5   Top-Down Management: Effects on the Family

Introduction

Every adult needs a child to teach, it's the way adults learn.[40]

Frank A. Clark

The survival of any society depends largely on what the people within the society can produce to build their standard of living. It also depends somewhat on the strength of the family unit. Families interested in improving their communities ultimately help establish community values, laws, commerce, medical facilities, education, and entertainment. Through these and other efforts, cultural patterns and community stability develop. In order to create functional communities, people residing in them must be motivated toward doing those things that are best for the community to develop. This effort must include developing responsible children.

In the business and educational worlds we just surveyed, it was shown how today's problem with the top-down style of management is catching up with them. The same is happening in the family unit. The subtle psychological changes that have taken place in our society that are affecting motivation in business and education are also affecting the way our families are managed and how children are raised. Our traditional ideas about human development are now often the basis of family discord. The ideas include questionable methods of teaching and motivating, disciplining, communicating, rewarding and punishing, and building self-esteem and self-reliance.

Families in the primitive era of human development could well have been the human source that started the not-so-effective style of motivation that all American institutions are now challenged to change. Many of us have seen pictures of a primitive woman being dragged by her hair by primitive man. This demonstrates a law of the jungle or the might-is-right attitude. The use of power and punishment evolved early. Even to this day, many parents defend their autocratic methods of human development with the well-known "Spare the rod, spoil the child."

Many parents would disregard the comment of Socrates, which we remember was "Violence is a confession of ignorance," and continue to use corporal punishment on their children. It is even worse for America as a developing country that parents are not shown proper, research-based methods of motivation.

Dominance over an individual and methods to force compliance and obedience used to gain some type of order and provide basic needs could be observed in early groups of the human race. Some teen-agers, many workers, some battered wives (and husbands), and many abused children of today might say that things have not improved much. The male is often looked upon as the head of the household, and many believe they have to make the major decisions for a family. From this type organization, young people learn early on that a top-down, power-laden form of management is best in order to control the behaviors of others. Most families are set up on a hierarchy basis, at least to the extent that the parents allow little input from their offspring as far as how things will be managed.

The Hierarchy . . . Not Just in Business and Education

There is little difference in the way people are motivated in America's families and how they are motivated in our businesses or schools. The majority of families can still be viewed as traditional as they use the top-down, power-oriented approach to motivate, discipline, and develop people. This form of management has become as devastating to family life as it has to productivity in business and to learning in education.

Young people in families leave us many messages, just as our students and workers do, that say they do not like the way they are being managed. This should not be surprising. Writing about parents in a book about raising a responsible child, Dr. Don Dinkmeyer and Dr. Gary McKay stated, "Their experience as children in autocratic homes and schools have not equipped them to function democratically."[41] Hence, parents in the United States often develop youngsters who carry on the top-down style of motivating and managing people. It is a form of our vicious circle that keeps power-based management thriving as democratic methods take a back seat.

It was mentioned in the section on business that we have managers who sap the spirit and energy of workers, tear down self-images of workers, and demoralize them even though they might not be trying to do so. Parents are accustomed to using our spirit killers, and they begin to hinder proper personality development at a young age.

Part of the management structure of business developed from attempts to form order in families. Young in families were dependent on older, stronger, and wiser people to provide the basic needs. These needs were food, clothing, safety, and, just a step below in importance, love, acceptance, and a feeling of being worthwhile. It was families who started businesses as early America was taking shape. Forms of management and orderliness were originated for a reasonable existence in family life and were transferred to businesses as they developed.

From this loose form of organizational "orderliness," the hierarchy management structure we know today emerged. The early business management structure created reasonably fair guidelines for orderliness, and people, "seeking meaning," benefited from building the system. Through necessity they cooperated with each other as they did in families.

The inability we have developed to get the best out of people had not yet taken a stranglehold on our country in the early 1900s. Perhaps the quest for survival from 1492 to the early 1900s provided enough meaning for the majority that hierarchical controls and external motivation were more tolerable than they are today.

Many people now believe that we have become greedy, that there is a need to return to a more cooperative spirit that early America enjoyed. We know that refined research in management skills is telling us that people in our institutions, including the family, are interested in the psychological aspects of their development. They want a more democratic form of management because they know true productivity cannot exist without input from those doing the work.

The family was once a strength in America's development, but now many of our leaders, especially in social science, law, and psychology, believe the family strength we have enjoyed is beginning to crumble. It may be in jeopardy because the fast-growing business world has had a tremendous effect on families. Some blame the decline of the family on both parents having to work to support the family, but the decline has deeper roots.

Our productivity, which dictates the growth of our economy and our standard of living, has not given us the luxury of allowing one parent to stay home. The real reason for the decline of the family is the result of the attitude we have developed about motivating our people. The humiliation, embarrassment, and ridicule that top-down management uses in trying to motivate people in business is duplicated by parents who are trying to motivate their young people. Tension is created in such environments, and motivation and development suffers.

Management in our schools took a similar path as management in business, and it must also take responsibility for transferring poor motivational and development techniques to parents.

Families are small societies just like businesses and schools. It is essential they help develop personalities that will put forth the effort to maintain orderliness and help America be competitive. Dr. Dinkmeyer and Dr. McKay gave us some insights as to why our institutions should be developing self-reliant people who maintain their own order within the regulations of our society. They commented, "Observing the rules of order holds top priority in any established society, for without order chaos and eventual self-destruction can be the only course."[41]

Has our system of developing our people become so tainted that we are approaching an era where chaos and eventual self-destruction is going to happen sometime in the twenty-first century? Many people, including some astute social observers, believe the chaos that poorly developed, underachieving, ruthless people bring to a society is upon us. We talk about things such as the taking back of our streets, metal detectors at school entrances, and the greed shown when companies lay off thousands of people yet the chief executive officers are given hefty bonuses.

Parents of today, if they are to escape the tornado-like path of poor development of their children, must understand the skills of human development mentioned regarding managing in business and teaching in education. Parents, like managers and teachers, cannot use autocratic, old-fashioned methods to effectively teach democratic values and self-reliance because such methods create disorder. When we lose our orderliness as a society, we become vulnerable.

A few items of disorderliness that lead to our vulnerability are drug and alcohol problems, suicide, apathy, illicit sex, and poor work and study habits in our young people. We can add runaways, gangs, and cult worshipping, stealing, vandalism and problems with self-image, self-motivation and non-acceptance of laws and authority. All can be chalked up to how we go about managing and motivating people.

Youngsters have been telling us through the behavior they display that our schools need radical change. Parents are an intricate part of the hierarchy structure as far as young people are concerned, and they should observe more closely to find clues from them to help them fully develop. To repeat, Frank A. Clark said, "Every adult needs a child to teach, it's the way adults learn." The hierarchical structure in families is not paying enough attention to those things the young people are trying to, in an indirect way, teach us about being more democratic.

There is no doubt the autocratic attitudes transmitted to our youth in our families carry over as they attend school and begin work as adults. This makes it more difficult for all concerned in an institution to create a democratic atmosphere because the top-down approach will still prevail. It takes great leaders to instill democratic human development principles into institutions.

For young people who have yet to become involved in the world of work, our family structure and our schools have the most effect on their development. It has been shown how schools can adversely affect young people. Following are several things that can happen in families when they fail to institute good human development techniques and instead allow our spirit killers to become a big part of the family atmosphere.

Participatory or Non-Participatory Families?

The family is where values, prejudices, frames of reference, assumptions, feelings of worth, and other aspects of belief systems originate. If an autocratic, top-down approach of managing people is taught in the family, it will be difficult to help those people who emerge from this environment to learn more democratic, less threatening, less stress-producing ways of relating to others. Such development is later a deterrent to these people as they attempt to motivate others.

As so far noted, Americans lean toward coercion and discouragement for motivation. Dr. Dinkmeyer and Dr. McKay agree:

> *Our autocratic tradition emphasizing punishment and reward has trained us to prod and nag rather than encourage.*[41]

Parents prod and nag often. Families participating in democratic methods of motivation could eliminate much of the prodding and nagging. The nagging often leads to spirit killers such as sarcasm, embarrassment, coercion, and ridicule, which in turn can lead to loss of self-esteem. It is not good management. Once these culprits arrive, the energy and enthusiasm dissipates in families, and they become dysfunctional. We have too many mismanaged, dysfunctional families in our country.

"You are starting to act like a baby." "Just wait until you want something from me." "You aren't even responsible enough to clean your room; how can I trust you with the car?" "Do that one more time and you are grounded." "I don't suppose you are going to study any this weekend either. How do you expect to get the grades we expect of you?" "Your brother could do that when he was six years old, and you are almost nine." "Sure, I'll give you five dollars for every A you get, but I don't think you are going to make much." The same autocratic language, the same attitude that we use to motivate people in their jobs or in their classrooms, is used in our homes.

Democratic environments, where people best develop their talents, can only become commonplace in America when we devise a system whereby more parents learn to change their erroneous beliefs about human development and motivation.

Ethnic origins, backgrounds, family traditions, and cultural differences should never be allowed to supersede good human development and motivational skills. Americans have devised ways to ignore these skills, and it is obvious that people from other cultures who have chosen to raise families in America have also devised ways to ignore true motivational techniques.

There is no question that many parents are now aware of the benefits of being more democratic. The problem is, they have difficulty creating this desired family atmosphere because of their traditional family, school, and work development. Being too permissive or too autocratic is a constant source of frustration for most parents. Instilling the essential self-discipline into young people by inspiring them and encouraging them is a skill that involves the successful sharing of accomplishments, failures, and feelings. It is a managing skill parents need to improve upon soon if we are to enter the twenty-first century confident of our ability to bring about true productivity through true motivation.

The right blend of advice, praise and criticism, questioning, and other aspects of communication, can build trust, confidence, courage, and intrinsic motivation in young people. Comments such as, "I want you to clean the garage and mow the backyard," could be changed by eliminating the powerful

"*I*" and saying, "The garage needs to be cleaned, and the backyard needs to be mowed. Can you finish those jobs while I patch the driveway and mow the front?" This is the language of a participatory family, not one torn apart by powerful language.

The above example does not demand obedience or compliance. It is not the old tradition of telling young people what to do. Its tone is more of "I could use some help," or "Can we do this together?" Life together is more of a "we" venture. Parents, like managers and teachers, fail when they use their power to get things done. David Ewing wrote,

---

To the extent that you have to rely on the authority of your position, you're a questionable manager.[42]

It is often said that young people do not have respect for authority. When young people discover that authority is being used on them in an ineffective and abusive manner, they see the people who are supposed to be leading them as failing them. The failure of an authority figure to properly motivate often brings a sense of despair to those who know they need guidance and development from that person.

School counselors see many defeated parents whose management skills in the use of praise and criticism, providing internal motivation, responding to feeling and giving up power are poorly developed. It has usually meant several years of bickering and fighting with their offspring while the young people were in school.

The inability to give and take, not to demand, not to dominate, is costly for most parents. These incapacities, along with being too permissive, often create unwanted dependence and are the most vital issues parents face in influencing their young people to do their best.

Many young people, tired of the top-down power, threats, and dominance, seek subtle revenge by performing poorly in school. Others maintain their grades, but dress in strange ways or choose different hairstyles. More extreme measures of rebellion consist of putting pins and rings in their noses or ears. Many try drugs and alcohol or running away as a way to deliver a message that they are not participating in their development and are being coerced.

The suicide rate among young people is always high because many of them become unhappy with themselves. Tired of being dominated by other people, young people often assume a position of being demotivated and feeling inadequate to themselves and those around them. In essence, these young people are using their own power to counteract the abusive power used on them.

Time and time again parents fight with their young people from the early grades through high school. Later, after the youngsters go to college, find a job, or go into the service, parents discover they have lost their power, and the relationships are, miraculously, much improved. Dr. Thomas Gordon stated right in the middle of his book *P.E.T.—Parent Effectiveness Training,* "If parents could learn one thing from this book, I wish it were this: Each and every time they force a child to do something by using power or authority, they deny that child a chance to learn self-discipline and self-responsibility."[43]

Using authority and demanding obedience and compliance are common errors in managing children. This demeaning system eventually has an effect on our schools and workplaces by creating autocratic people who work in them. Our national circumstances have become deplorable because we now know better ways to develop our people, but we are not using these methods. Creativity, originality, and a high degree of energy are attributes of people who follow their own dictates. We can do, and will need to do, a better job of developing these people by taking actions to help parents learn proven human development skills.

Authoritarian leadership creates the destructive behavior we see so many young people demonstrate. Psychologists teach that if we can create people who have a sense of worthwhileness, they will do things that are worthwhile for themselves and society. Dr. Dinkmeyer and Dr. McKay wrote,

> *A child who sees himself as worthwhile and useful has no need to develop destructive patterns of behavior.*[43]

In some respects, the parenting process is the most challenging of all processes associated with managing and motivation because parents have so much at stake. Since they have more to lose, the pressure mounts, and they often turn to autocratic methods to get results. Of course, this action correlates to the action autocratic managers in business employ when they want results now and are not concerned with the long term.

Perhaps Dr. Dinkmeyer and Dr. McKay said it best when it comes to understanding the proper process in moving young people from dependence to independence:

> *We see discipline as growth from dependence to independence, which is a product of intrinsic motivation.*[43]

Parents must be able to speak a language that instills intrinsic motivation. The language must be one void of power and all of our spirit killers if it is to take hold and help develop a young person so he is forward moving, seeking meaning, responsible to himself and others, and happy within himself.

Special Language for Preventative Parenting

Preventative parenting can be compared to preventative medicine. If we eat the right foods, exercise, and avoid smoking, we can prevent health problems. Preventative parenting consists of parents learning the special language which produces intrinsic motivation to children.

The term *special language* has been used so much up to this point that it should be defined in more detail. It is a way of arranging our words so we do not create an autocratic environment for those with whom we are trying to live, work, or teach. It is a way of structuring our communication so it is void of power and threats, and is more influential. It is designed to help people become self-reliant and develop the type of people a society needs to maintain orderliness so the freedoms of everyone are not infringed upon. By using power-filled, coercive language, we are developing people full of apathy, greed, resentment, and anger that translates into violence, revenge, and dependence . . . and more trouble in the twenty-first century.

Everyone attempting to learn how to be more democratic and more encouraging must go through a painful period of ridding himself of autocratic speech patterns. These patterns were first developed by a culturally ingrained attitude in significant people around them. The ingrained belief system must go through a resounding reevaluation before the words can come out more empathetically, encouragingly, and democratically.

The term *special language* was first used by Peters and Waterman when they reported that good companies in the United States had a common characteristic, namely a "special language." The language was motivational in its content. It was not one where power and authority were the mainstay of top-down management. It was a language that allowed people to participate, one that was always able to encourage people to do their best. Spirit-killing phrases and power-filled words were just not present in these companies. A congenial, stress-free, harmonious environment was enjoyed, and productivity was evident. The halo effect was ever present.

It might be better to call this new language the "different language" because no new words are used; they are just arranged differently. Calling it a different language might be a better way to signal to people that we have to change the way we go about talking to each other if we are going to motivate each other better and prevent America from being at risk in the twenty-first century.

The vicious circle described in the section on education, in which parents and educators abuse the language to motivate young people, is alive and well in the parenting process. More often than not, the parents of parents passed on pet authoritarian remarks that help complete the vicious circle in families. Even when parents take some training in the way they talk with their youngsters, their overall attitude must change or the young people will figure out the authoritarian attitude is present. They will feel the power and strike back against it.

In trying to get good, consistent efforts out of young people, all those working with them must realize that the phrase, "We cannot fool a child," is accurate. When a young child says, "Let me do it, Mommy," the child is expressing a desire to be independent. If the parent goes ahead and does something that the child could do for himself, the authoritarian attitude is felt by the child. Too much of this feeling injected into a child as the child grows is detrimental to the child's development and personality. The special language would tell the child, "Oh, I'm sure you can do it. Go ahead."

Leaders in all institutions respond to events instead of feelings. When this happens, feelings are minimized. This is especially true of parents because young people express their feelings to them on an ongoing basis. Our top-down language has taught, or forced, many working adults to keep feelings in, and we have seen unexpressed feelings explode into violence far too often in our society. Minimized, neglected feelings in schools, at work, and in families are turning America into a feelingless society. Heinous crimes are committed with little remorse. It may be difficult to comprehend how our autocratic language contributes to developing people with personalities capable of committing such crimes, but it does.

Following is a common example of how a father might, unwittingly, minimize the feelings of his son. One such incident is not important, but constant minimizing of feelings can be lethal.

When a teen-age boy brought home his first grade report from high school, the father, who had some minimal training in the special language asked, "How do you feel about your grade report?"

His son said, "I got an A in English, three Bs, and two Cs. I got a C in Biology. I don't like my teacher very much. All in all, I think I studied hard and did pretty good."

The father said, "What could you do to make them better?"

His son replied, "Take easier classes."

The father missed the feeling his boy was sending to him. He responded to the event (the grade report) and included in his response things the special language would not have us do. He gave an opinion, a judgment, or analysis, and evaluated the situation from his perspective.

Many people trying to change their attitudes from autocratic to democratic do not see where the communication pattern in this example could be improved upon. A better response by the father might have been, "It sounds as though you believe you made a good effort and are pretty satisfied with your report." This response does not minimize feeling. It provides a chance for the son to look at his effort and see if it is possible to improve because *he* wants to, not because his father wants him to. It keeps the concentration of the conversation on the boy and not on the wishes of the father. It is a democratic response that is more apt to keep the discussion going. It gives the father a chance to get the boy to look at himself, which he is trying to do. The son ended hope of a discussion by saying the way he could improve was to "take easier classes."

The problem in the above example is that the father may know his boy could do better in school. The question then becomes, how does the father motivate the young man to do better? Nagging and prodding probably will not do it, and the use of power, fear, ridicule, pleas, or punishment will not either. Responding in a consistent way so the boy can look at his behavior and knows someone cares about him is the only way the grades are going to improve. One thing is for certain, the grades will improve only if the boy chooses to make the effort to improve them.

The special language for preventative parenting must, for the most part, eliminate logic, which seems to many parents to be their sound sense based on their experiences. Experienced counselors know that using logic to change someone's behavior seldom changes that behavior. Instead, reflecting thoughts and feelings back to someone for their evaluation is the research-based way to change behavior. Overusing questions, analysis, and confrontations seldom accomplish the results that are needed for good development. Making assumptions and using external motivation as well as sending unclear messages, praising, manipulating, and using sarcastic put-downs are a waste of communication time in trying to develop young people.

These errors in personal communication, common in parenting, undermine self-esteem, the greatest of all motivators. Trust cannot be built up when all of these autocratic spirit killers are woven into daily communication with young people. Parents, teachers, and managers must begin to understand that the simple little words we use everyday loom big in terms of what our people will do with their lives. The special language can be used to develop special people.

Running Away . . . from the Hierarchy

Thousands of young people run away from home each year. There is little doubt the most common cause is one all Americans have heard: a breakdown in communication.

In modern America, most families can survive some autocratic language; but when it is used over and over as a form of motivation, it will have deleterious effects. If the language in the family is void of words that encourage, and promote independence and self-esteem, trouble could be brewing. It thwarts enthusiasm by neglecting democratic principles and words that create independent functioning. Young people run away from such environments because, in struggling to understand themselves, they know this atmosphere is not right for their development.

Recommending that a special language should be practiced in all homes does not mean that parents cannot get angry, offer advice, or even confront their offspring.

A life without confrontation is meaningless.

Socrates

Most parents tend to use confrontations as their standard bearer, and they become ineffective. Some young people run away because they do not believe that their parents, who constantly confront them, are genuine or real people in terms of relating to them.

Some of the strange things our young adults do are simply attempts to find a more comfortable environment in which to live. Our autocratic, unintentional verbal muggings create environments in our homes and schools from which our young people want to escape. Often, running away means to them that, no matter what happens, they will find a better existence. We should look at the messages young people leave behind as serious clues to consider if we are going to change our approach to motivating them. We cannot get the best out of our young people if they keep running away from us.

"You will follow the rules in this house or you can't live in this house," is a rather common hierarchical comment given by many parents to their offspring. We often forget in working with young people that they are motivated or demotivated in the same way as their parents. They also like to have input into those things that happen in a family that have impact on their lives.

Many parents belong to unions at work because they want more input into the rules under which they work. It was noted in the section on business that workers in unions are often seeking psychological needs to be met by management. Youngsters are doing the same thing when they rebel against communication patterns of parents that rob them of meeting these important needs. Parents fail to understand that their youngsters have similar feelings about the lack of a democratic atmosphere to settle differences at home.

At any given moment, over one million runaways are on the streets of our cities. These are discouraged youngsters, and their discouragement leads to strange, unproductive behavior in our society. Many of these young people will become drug addicts, prostitutes, thieves, scam artists, car-jackers, and other cast-offs of society. Their behavior will cost us much more than it would have cost us to prevent the behavior through rigorous parent training programs. As the twenty-first century approaches, we need to take more interest in how we go about managing our young people. Until recently, we had more intricate computer systems and high-tech methods of finding stolen automobiles than we did missing young people.

Force-outs may be a better term for youths who run away from home or who are kicked out or who drop out of school. It is a national disaster that our institutions, which should be set up to provide for the needs of young people, are failing at such a rate that, unless something changes, America cannot survive in the twenty-first century. If we add runaways and dropouts to the people on welfare, to the ranks of homeless and the unemployed, we might ask this question: what does a government do to cause such a condition in which it is not getting better results out of its people? As pointed out once before, our two major political parties endorse human development policies that are demotivational.

Is not the real test of a government's effectiveness the things it does to provide for the needs of its down-and-out people? Is not the government of any society responsible for the conditions under which people governed by it are living? It is a fact that we are beginning to lag behind other major countries in implementing into our society better human development programs.

In some countries, a portion of each paycheck received by a worker is used for children and family services. It is alarming that one quarter of American children live in poverty. The United States is not only a world leader in runaways, but also homeless children and children lacking nutrition and overall childcare. It is poor management of human resources. Lip service for these issues was provided again when "family values" recently became political rhetoric. We are running away from our children more than they are running away from us.

It is well known that governments in other countries, especially those in Europe, pay more attention to the development of children than the United States does. In America, helping youngsters develop becomes a political football. An article in *Time* magazine titled "Where Children Come First" alluded to this dilemma. Rae Grad, executive director of the national Commission to Prevent Infant Mortality, may have summed up the national attitude best:

> The money would come if we believed in our heart of hearts that children were important to this country.[44]

It must be considered healthy on the part of young people in some families to run away from a frightening environment that is filled with physical or sexual abuse. Physical abuse has to be reported in most states, but will we ever get to the point where emotional abuse, which can be just as devastating, will have to be reported? It is doubtful the spirit-killing words can be totally eliminated, but training programs could help if properly set up at work, schools, and other community centers.

The special language could cut down on runaways because there would not be anything from which to run. Life in the family could be fun, pleasant, and meaningful. Young people could be given quality moments to remember through family activities and language that build encouragement. Parents can do these things whether they are rich or poor.

It may be that a special language evolves in the poor and depressed families because some parents figure out that this is the one way to give their children a chance to compete in our society. They build them up with love, kindness, and encouragement that is hard to beat down, no matter how demoralizing school systems and workplaces are.

Young people, full of the human spirit, are resilient and therefore can absorb some of our imperfect language and imperfect forms of discipline. There is, however, a point of no return; when that point is reached, it will cause them to rebel in the ways we are so vividly reminded of in the media each day.

Do We Manage Young People into Drugs, Alcohol, and Sex?

The temporary comfort our young people find in which to get away from the spirit killers in homes and schools are often drugs and alcohol, getting high or being sexually promiscuous. These escape mechanisms are still only looked upon as inadmissible evidence regarding ineffective top-down management of young people. They could be telling us something is terribly wrong with the way we go about helping young people reach their highest potential.

Leaders in institutions, including parents, seem to have an acquired belief that other people or other institutions are the real forces behind young people escaping into a make-believe existence. We are all in this together, and we should be more concerned that our system of human development, motivation, and management of people causes so many problems. There are no longer destructive forces of human development in our system that we cannot identify. If Americans can identify a problem, they can usually make a good effort to rid themselves of it. We have not made that effort since we have almost totally neglected the research that tells us how we could improve in managing our people.

Parents do, of course, try to rationalize the causes of drug, alcohol, and sex abuse by blaming these tragedies on our self-designed cop-outs of television, peer pressure, a vacillating economy, and tedious world situations. Rationalizing a problem away is a favorite trick of any hierarchy. We have an abundance of great young people who watched television, were subjected to peer pressure, and lived in an up-and-down economy. What saved them from experiencing the misery of drugs and alcohol and other escape mechanisms? They were fortunate enough to have people around them who built them up so they might one day become self-sufficient.

Our style of developing and managing people should not be comforting to us as we head into the twenty-first century. The U.S.S.R. officials keep looking for something other than their oppressive management style in hope of finding a cause for the tremendous waste of their people. The ever-increasing alcohol abuse and high crime rate in that country signifies that their government has not provided opportunities for its people to find meaning. People there do not like the way they are being governed. The drug and alcohol abuse found in America's young people is an escape from top-down governing in homes, schools, and businesses. In the same way, the citizens in the U.S.S.R. try to escape a top-down government that robs them of meaning.

Many Americans believe that inherited traits cause our young people to resort to drugs, alcohol, and sex, and that eliminating the autocratic managing style will not solve the problem. Using genetics as an excuse to justify the effects of top-down management may be the worst of all cop-outs.

In addition to genetics being used as an excuse to keep alive top-down governing, peer pressure is often identified as a major factor in perpetuating the destructive behavior of young people. In some respects, parents and schools may be doing a tremendous disservice to our society by claiming that peer pressure is the number one source in determining whether or not a youngster turns to drugs, alcohol, and sex as a means of meeting needs.

These abuses may not necessarily be caused by peer pressure, but instead by domineering, autocratic, feelingless systems of motivation found in our families and schools. Peers who attempt to influence others into drug, alcohol, and sex abuse have first been abused by the system. If that were not the case, they would not feel the need to gain companionship and acceptance through the subtle coercive methods they devise. Neither the parents nor officials in the school systems see their methods of motivation and management as contributing to peers trying to convince others to escape from hierarchical controls.

Peer pressure should be looked upon as another clue, a symptom that something has gone wrong with our ability to supply good psychological development in young people. It is a spirit killer because we do not recognize it as a force that prevents us from implementing good understanding of the principles of human development and motivation.

The drug, alcohol, and sex culture in which so many of our young people are wasting away is not the form of orderliness our country should take pride in. Our country's orderliness is certainly out of kilter when we see our paramedics spend so much time transporting our young people who have abused drugs to local hospitals. We fail to realize that how we go about achieving order in our society is the real reason we have so much cocaine, heroin, crack, and marijuana in our country. If we do not learn to build self-reliance in our young people, we cannot possibly build enough hospitals in the twenty-first century to house drug abusers.

The tension we create with our top-down, autocratic management is welcomed by the drug dealers. The dealers love the tension created in our society by a government that does little to prevent the chaos that our system of developing people creates.

It is just so difficult for enough people of influence to understand that our attitudes regarding how to get the best out of people are causing drug dealers to swarm all over America.

Now the dealers are even able to push the drugs into small rural communities, which was unheard of forty years ago.

Our drug culture will grow as long as the tension created by our autocratic form of managing and motivating people continues to exist. We must understand that our spirit killers, those poorly arranged words, have so entrenched themselves into our society that they now cause so much tension that there is talk of legalizing the drugs to relieve the tension. What a tremendous victory for the spirit killers.

It is common in America for parents to take their young people to drug abuse centers. There are some good centers, but many lack the communication skills to build self-esteem and confidence in our young people to the point that they can rely on themselves instead of drugs. Once released, they are not strong enough to deal with the autocratic, oppressive system of parenting, teaching, or managing. The tension again gets the best of them, and they return to drugs to rid themselves of the tension. If we, as a proud nation of people, do become more interested in developing our youth, more money must be put into training people who can help young people become self-reliant and contribute to society. We cannot continue to invest money and give jobs to untrained people who may be contributing to the downfall of young people because of their autocratic backgrounds.

It is demoralizing, but drugs, alcohol, and sex are just a few of the ways young people run away from the hierarchy family structure in an attempt to meet their needs. Following are other ways.

Gangs and Cults

An ex-gang member in Chicago was asked what he thought could be done to prevent young people from joining gangs. He said, "Communication, parents communicating better." Most of the time, vulnerable young people cannot explain what they need from parents other than "better communication."

Young people often have difficulty putting into words exactly what they are feeling. For instance, they seldom tell us their feelings are being minimized, that they want to set their own goals and have some freedom to make mistakes without being verbally abused. They have been made to believe that it is important for them to do things so their parents or teachers will be proud of them. They are not able, because of the hierarchical management system, to understand that it is more important for them to do things so they will be proud of themselves.

When parents are asked by television or newspaper reporters what they think of the outstanding accomplishments of their youngster, they will invariably say, "We are very proud of him (or her)." The young people often say, "I just wanted to make my parents proud of me." Intrinsic motivation follows a different path. If there is one thing parents should be proud of, it is the fact that their children are doing things that they—the children—are proud of doing.

Gangs and cults flourish in America more so today than ever before. People are joining their ranks because their needs are not being met in the mainstream of our society. Young people who have had their feelings minimized to the point of no return seek out the basic need of belonging. Parents can relay so many discouraging messages through the autocratic system of communicating that it only takes a few years for them to kill the spirit of a young person. Once the spirit is wounded, anything can happen in terms of psychological turmoil. Threats, ridicule, coercion, embarrassment, fear, humiliation, belittlement, and other verbal arrows that pierce the hearts of our young people are the real culprits that cause our gangs to flourish.

We might suspect that the needs of security and social connectiveness are a high priority when a young person decides to affiliate with a gang. Safety should not be looked upon as just a physical need to be secure. It should be looked upon as a psychological need as well.

Autocratic, top-down management techniques produce tremendous conflict between parents and their offspring, and many young people are managed into the streets. The government then comes along and appropriates money to build gyms, swimming pools, and playgrounds, to form programs like midnight basketball leagues to keep the youngsters off the streets. Politicians can then have the facilities or programs named after them for their stopping of gangs from spreading, but these facilities and programs are not the appropriate deterrent for gangs.

Of course, the government is going to say that it does not have the right to tell parents how to raise their children, but then it blames the parents for producing young people who are not disciplined enough to follow the regulations set up by our society. The time will come where programs will have to identify at an early age those youngsters who are not getting the proper form of motivation at home. Even now, children are placed in Head Start programs where they are supposed to get caught up in their development so they might have a chance for success in school. Programs like Head Start can fail if the teachers in them use the same form of autocratic motivation and discipline that caused the youngsters to fall behind in the first place.

Thousands of gang shootings take innocent lives every year. Our spirit-killing form of motivation can once again claim victory. Gang violence is a reflection of our ignorance and non-caring attitudes about how our young people are developing. It is a national tragedy that can only get worse unless we make drastic changes in our approach to human development.

Gangs are beginning to affect the freedoms of many Americans. We, with our autocratic system of human development, puncture the spirit of our young people; then they devise a way to take our freedoms from us. They congregate at malls and fast-food places for social connectiveness—a need—and citizens avoid going there. The top-down-managed government then passes an ordinance forbidding youngsters to gather at these places, so they go elsewhere.

Before long, the gangs are forced underground, but the members are still seething because they do not have a true sense of belonging to anything except the gang. Their behavior will likely worsen because feelings minimized for a long time usually explode. Improvement in our system is needed to recognize these explosive feelings and diffuse them before the emotions of these young people finally erupt. Most community leaders "fight" gangs and advertise "zero tolerance" for them. As long as communities "fight" with gangs, there will be gangs because the members' original fight came about because needs were not being met by family or some organization in the community.

Gang members see the community leaders' attitudes as only an extension of a system that deprived them of having their needs met in the first place. It is almost as though we believe that young people are responsible for their own needs even though they have never been taught democratic ways to arrive at those needs. To reiterate, it is impossible to teach young people democratic ways of functioning by using autocratic methods so commonly found in our institutions.

Psychological needs, such as recognition, are implanted in young people by saying something like, "You should be proud of the way you played. Your rebounding and shooting was amazing." If they hear, "You played a good game, but you will never make it in high school if you don't hit the books and practice," it is not as encouraging. The first comment has a better chance of motivating the youngster, whereas the second does not allow him to enjoy the present success and understand that he can be proud of his skills. The first comment may help the youngster to feel so good about himself that he may want to repeat the behavior that was recognized.

Fighting against gangs may be politically correct, but gangs need to be dispersed by way of fitting gang members into schools, jobs, and activities, and associating them with people who can give meaning to their lives by the way they motivate them.

We need to use all of the research and other resources in our culture to discover why gangs meet needs that should be met by families and other institutions in a vibrant, functioning society. How far into the twenty-first century can we continue to proclaim it is the right of parents to develop a child the way they see fit even if that development defies research and is destructive to the child and society? Just as they are managed into drugs, alcohol, and sex, young people are managed into gangs and cults.

Some gangs have responded to programs in which they take part in building up their community instead of tearing it down. Programs of this type meet the needs of gang members who are starved for things such as gratification, being on a winning team, doing something meaningful, and developing pride in something. It gives the young people some hope that they may have not had before. If the people working with gang members can respond to their comments and the feelings they give out by going beyond their words and arranging words so the young people know they are accepted and are worthwhile, a major hurdle will have been overcome. Delinquent young people are not born delinquent; they learn to become delinquent.

There will always be people in our society who have had their spirits diminished to the point it is almost impossible to bring them back. Because of this, we will always need police, jail, and prison wardens, judges, and other law enforcement officials because we cannot hope for utopia. These officials, with the proper training, can improve on helping the people they come in contact with to understand the reasons why they are there in the first place. They can serve to remind people about the good principles of motivation, leadership, and management instead of just dispensing justice and adding to the reputation of a hierarchical system so many people rebel against.

Gang members know that painting graffiti on walls and causing people to be inconvenienced is a way of showing power. It is abused power similar to the power used on them that caused them to turn off about our society. They know that broken windows and flat tires have to be repaired. Gangs exist for the exact reason that Dr. Thomas Gordon told us years ago, but our government, businesses, schools, and parents do not place much faith in warnings of those who have studied the research in human development, leadership, motivation, and management. Once again, Dr. Gordon expertly informed us, "It is inevitable that coercive power generates the very forces that eventually will combat it and bring about a more equitable balance of power."[48]

Is it not time that we see gangs as one of those forces that is combating autocratic power? They are generating forces that they hope will bring about a more equitable balance of power.

Gangs are unions for young people.

As in the business world, unions are caused; they do not just happen. Unions are votes against power-oriented management in most companies. Gangs are votes against power-oriented parents, schools, and governments. Like members of a labor union, gang members are seeking needs, both psychological and physiological. Most communities are now beginning to feel the power that gangs have obtained. Adults in well-managed companies have learned to cooperate with each other to meet common goals, often without unions. It is more difficult for authorities to work with young people and create the same cooperative, powerless atmosphere in our communities that these well-managed companies enjoy.

The cults thriving in America often serve a slightly different form of escape for our need-searching youth. Many of our youth have been made to be dependent on others. Some parents are so afraid of their offspring making mistakes that they do everything for them or use power to tell them what they must do. The young people get accustomed to their behavior being controlled. They have little chance to develop self-discipline because the powers that be make every decision for them. They become followers.

The cults now flourishing find it easy to take in people who have suffered from autocratic forms of development that makes them followers. Behavior control in a cult is a little more subtle than that which parents often provide. Cults give the impression that their paradise-like management will give young people the opportunity to escape the oppressiveness of parents. Like many of our schools and businesses, on the surface they look great and seemingly will provide a need-fulfilling environment where youngsters can express themselves and enjoy freedom to do meaningful things.

A vivid example of how we develop dependent people is the tragedy of the massacres orchestrated by cult leader Reverend Jim Jones in Jonestown, Guyana. He persuaded 900 people, mostly Americans, to commit suicide by drinking poison. He accomplished this by one reason. These people were followers; they were dependent upon Jones to make decisions for them. Few Americans will forget the horrifying fire in Waco, Texas that ended the religious cult of David Koresh and his followers. Top-down management principles claimed more victims.

A few people survived in Guyana, and psychiatrists who examined them reported that these people were like zombies, almost void of feelings. Yes, our spirit-killing form of communication and our power-oriented, top-down style of motivation and management can do this to people. We do not realize how much power our top-down system of managing human beings holds over people.

Hitler, Jim Jones, David Koresh, and many other unscrupulous, high-profile leaders throughout history have been able to convince large groups of people to join their controlled environments. It is an undeniable fact that gangs and cults flourish because our young people want to escape from other autocratic leaders, many of whom are teachers, parents, and managers. They do not fully understand that power and control are going to play a big part in any top-down managed organization, and their situations will not improve.

Gangs and cults will continue to thrive well into the twenty-first century. They will survive because we are not close to dealing with the lackluster human development methods that cause them to be a popular option for young people whose needs are not being met by traditional development.

Suicide

All people are born with a desire to live and develop a meaningful life. We have seen people endure essential organ transplants in an attempt "to keep on keeping on," as the saying goes. Many people have worked hard after personal tragedies to make their lives more meaningful. People so much want meaningful lives they will go to extremes to find them. Suicide means that the inborn trait to seek meaning has died. There is no will to go forward.

Whatever beliefs we hold about suicide, a discussion about it must be included in any attempt to identify the things we do and say in managing people that may help end the seeking of meaning for many people.

We can add our current statistics on suicide to those of our runaways, gang members, dropouts, and other people who are discouraged about their circumstances. Suicide may be the ultimate act of discouragement. It is another form of escape that our system of human development causes.

We should never deny that our top-down system of motivation and management in homes and elsewhere does not contribute to our suicide rates. Our autocratic, feelingless methods of motivation have had a hand in developing people discouraged enough to take their own lives. Minimized or completely avoided feelings can cause people to feel so badly about themselves that they no longer feel capable of attaining meaning in their lives.

When the following subheadings appeared in well-known newspapers throughout the country, many people might have wondered what caused the flame to go out in these young people:

*Traditional dad drives
2 Chinese teens to suicide*

Teen suicide rate leaps to new high

*Ridicule and failure
pushed boy to kill himself*

What caused these youngsters to finally say to themselves, "I give up"? Let us keep in mind that discouragement is the major force behind most anti social behavior. It can often lead to drastic acts. It leads to deviant behavior in some, a withdrawn posture in others, and a protesting behavior in many. We must include suicide as one of the protests against our spirit killers and our traditional forms of motivation, management, and human development.

Notice in one of the subheadings the word *traditional* is used to describe a father who drove two of his children to suicide. Another subheading informs us that it is possible for "ridicule and failure" to push people to such final acts of self-destruction.

People do not seek out ways to be discouraged and are not predisposed to be discouraged. Something in our society, in our culture, intervenes to bring about the discouragement. We are only fooling ourselves if we discard the fact that the way we relate to each other does not contribute to that discouragement. What degree of destruction that discouragement will bring is contingent upon how much encouragement is mixed in to help overcome the discouragement.

Listening and responding in a way that is encouraging and helps to build self-esteem is perhaps the most important aspect of preventing suicide. We know that people who feel good about themselves and their circumstances in life have no need to perform any destructive behaviors. Suicide is a destructive behavior because it has an effect on family members and other people around the discouraged person. The motivation to commit suicide is often thought to be for revenge or to show inadequate feeling about oneself. It is a final statement that says that too many important needs were not being met.

Through our autocratic management styles, it is possible to build into a personality so much despair that suicide becomes an alternative to the despair. Once too many feelings are rejected, there is a chance that an individual could begin to feel as though he is not worthwhile. It takes a leader with great skill in building people up to reverse this trend.

Suicide is no longer a statistic associated mostly with teenagers. Recent figures show that those sixty-five and older committed 20 percent of the suicides in the United States.

Suicide is always a shock to family members and other people around the victim. Self-esteem seems so fragile when a suicide happens, and it is probably more fragile than would-be leaders assume. It is often said of a suicide victim, "He just never gave the impression he would do something like that." Some victims do give clues that we are not very good at picking up, but most people give the impression that they are finding enough meaning in their lives to keep moving forward. Of course, many people do not want to give others the idea that they are not strong emotionally. To do so is a sign of weakness. Suicides inform us that it is sometimes difficult to detect when a person might be suffering from low self-esteem.

An expert on self-esteem, Gloria Blum wrote about it in *Impact*, the official publication of the Institute for Family Research and Education at Syracuse University. In the article titled "Myths and Realities of Self-Esteem," she wrote:

> Self-esteem is confidence and satisfaction with oneself. It involves learning how to give yourself approval, how to say, "I am okay." This is not something that comes automatically. It is something that must be learned.[46]

If self-esteem is to be learned, who is responsible for teaching it? We are! We can do it with our special language. The escapes from our traditional development that our young people look for manifest themselves in our society because we do not teach self-esteem like we should.

In her article, Gloria Blum wrote,

> When I was growing up, the aunties and uncles, and the mothers and fathers waited until children left the room before they would say, "Oh, isn't she wonderful, you can't believe it, she is so cute, she does so well in school. I'm so proud of her!", but we would never hear about it because they did not want us to get the big head. They thought that if they let us know how we were special, we would somehow become arrogant.[46]

It sounds like Gloria would like to have heard how proud her relatives were of her. It would have been better still if they could have said to her, "You have so much that you can be proud of." It is like we want to keep secret the building blocks of self-esteem. The old-fashioned thinking about self-esteem is still as prevalent in our society as the old-fashioned discipline techniques discussed earlier. They must be put to rest if we are to improve on motivating and developing our people in America in the twenty-first century.

Gloria Blum's comments shed some beautiful light on how we might get teenagers and people in our workforce to study and work harder:

> This myth about productivity is one that you may have come across if you work in any large office or organization: People perform better when they are reminded that they can be replaced. The attitude that goes with this is that we can get along without you, so you better keep in line. This is a myth, and is destructive to self-esteem. The reality is: "We are not complete without you." Doesn't that feel better? People perform best when they feel this attitude around them. It inspires people to think new ideas, and to take risks, and to put more into their work.[46]

Many parents, managers, and teachers in America still believe in the myth that Gloria Blum tries to dispel. They believe if they praise the good things a person does it will be detrimental to their growth. As we learned, too much praise can, indeed, be harmful. Building pride and self-confidence in someone is done differently than overusing praise. It is more expertly done by saying in many ways, "You can be proud of what you have done." To say, "I am proud of what you have done," is an evaluation of an individual's behavior and not as potent in building up self-esteem as saying, "You should be proud of what you have done." This type communication can make the person feel as though he did something for himself to be proud of instead of doing something to make other people proud.

Our mismanaged society has invented enough ways to "bring a kid down a peg or two." Schools and peers and bosses will probably see to that, so parents should spend their time building children up. It is a tough world out there sometimes, and we prepare people better to compete in it by building up their belief in themselves. Parents who autocratically try to keep their young people in line, as our bosses and teachers do in America, can actually create personalities that may try to escape the power through suicide or other ways.

When a suicide does happen, many of us just chalk it up to the ever-increasing stress produced in our society without taking a look at other factors in our society that could be behind such behavior. Gloria Blum cited some research that might give credence to our spirit killers causing stress and discouragement. She stated, "The findings indicate quite clearly that depression tends to be related to low self-esteem."[46] Top-down management philosophies, spirit-killing language, and old-fashioned discipline contribute heavily to low self-esteem.

Low self-esteem comes before a life-altering depression, and our spirit-killing words and discouraging motivational techniques come before low self-esteem. Rarely do we place blame on something we do that might cause someone to become so depressed he might consider suicide. No one individual should have to shoulder the blame for a suicide when we know that many people are, unwittingly, delivering discouraging words. It is difficult to see how small discouraging words can cause development of poor self-esteem that can work into stress, then discouragement, and then suicide or some other destructive behavior.

It is an error in human development to constantly tell young people what it is that they must correct to become successful. It is erroneous to dwell on negatives because it becomes discouraging. Gloria Blum noted in her writings that it is a myth that we must "first recognize someone's weaknesses or needs in order to design a plan of action to help them." She said such a plan "is designed to build on what they don't yet have," and went on to explain that we cannot build on holes or something people do not have; we have to build on strengths.[46] Every human being has some strength, some aptitude, some ability, some trait that can be used to build them up. Instead, in our society we look for weaknesses and spend our communication time trying to rid others of those weaknesses.

Ever hear of a three-year-old child committing suicide? It is rare, and this extremely low incidence rate should give us a clue that something in our society can produce discouragement so demeaning and so strong that it can wear on people as they get older. We may never get to hear the music of those people who are often reminded of their weaknesses. It is a sad situation for America that we have so many people who have been taught to view themselves in a negative way. Many who have learned to view themselves negatively develop a sense of worthlessness and eventually destroy themselves physically or emotionally.

Suicides, gangs, cults, and alcohol, drug, and sex abuse could all be cut to a minimum if we could only find leaders who would study what causes such tragedies in our society and then use their influence to develop community programs to put a stop to such waste of our human resources.

Child Abuse

Child abuse must be mentioned whenever motivation in America is the topic. It must also be mentioned when anyone is discussing how our human resources are wasted.

Self-discipline is, of course, the one ingredient that good human development strives to instill in our young people. In America today, there is confusion as to what good discipline is and is not. When does discipline end and child abuse begin? This is a legal question that must be defined in more rigid terms. Many parents see punishment as motivation to "set this kid straight" or "for your own good," or even, "You will thank me someday for spanking you now." "This will probably hurt me more than it will hurt you" is a common cop-out to use violence. The hierarchical, might-is-right attitude is perpetuated by our antiquated views of using violence to raise children in supposedly democratic ways.

Child abuse is just now coming to the forefront of public attention. It is just another of our multitude of clues that should tell us something is wrong with the way we teach people to develop other people. Stories appear daily in the nation's newspapers describing such things as torture, rape, molestings, beatings, and murder of children in families. Even priests and teachers have been convicted of child abuse. Some children have been sold like horses, and others have been left home alone for long periods of time.

Child abuse statistics should help us question our human developmental techniques and our laws and regulations that allow anyone to physically or emotionally abuse someone. It may well be that parents in the United States hit, slap, punch, shove, shake, and generally use force more than parents in any other country in the world. Child abuse is learned and is an extension of our autocratic approach to get people to do things. Autocratic, power-laden parents proclaim that "the kids will have to learn the hard way," or "kids have to learn to accept authority."

It is almost inconceivable that we believe that to hit a child does not teach that child to hit. We just do not understand that violence promotes violence. We think it does something good in terms of development. It does some good, but only in the short term, which is the same management attitude that has put many of our corporations and most of our schools in jeopardy. Short-term solutions to something that has been going on for a long time usually do not work. Such solutions cause problems down the road. There is little difference between teaching a child that violence is OK and unwittingly teaching that our autocratic language is OK. Both are done because they are so traditional. We are blinded to their effects on our society.

A Midwestern couple put their two daughters in a crawl space for punishment. Parents still put kids in dark closets or spank them to maintain order and "teach them a lesson." Belts and switches are still common weapons used to terrorize young people into compliance. If we believe that this type of human development does not contribute to our gang, drug, and alcohol problems, we are going to search forever for ways to solve these problems.

Resentment builds when power is abused. Parents are given so much power (just like an autocratic manager) that the legal rights of young people are only minimally discussed in the media when reporting on child abuse. Child abuse of all forms is perpetuated by a system that pays little attention to what adults do to children as long as what is done is within a family circle. Resentment builds in direct correlation to the verbal and physical abuse administered in families. The resentment built up from child abuse contributes greatly to poor work habits, a lack of respect for authority, and an increase in violent crime.

In some child abuse cases, especially those involving sexual abuse, we are now learning that the event was so terrifying that the young people repressed it for ten to twenty years. Such abuse can cause nightmares and develop anxiety in young people. Aggressive behavior may become a lifetime pattern for those who are victims of violent child abuse.

Research constantly tells us we are tinkering with self-esteem when we use any form of violence on a child. Part of the problem is that some parents who have used a minimal amount of violence, like a few spankings, spread the word that a "swat in the right place did not hurt our kids; they have turned out just fine." These kinds of references dash hopes in stopping those who carry physical abuse too far. Even the media outlets often sanction such ill-advised references to discipline and motivation.

Not much is said about what really causes our million-plus runaways, our drug and alcohol abusers, our dropouts, child abusers, and so on, because we come up with cop-outs to rationalize the idea that we cannot prevent these human tragedies. It is said that we cannot legislate moral codes, but we seldom attempt to install research-backed measures to prevent poor moral development in our schools, businesses, and families. It is obvious that preventative measures designed to stop child abuse would mean we should teach and monitor attitudes in our institutions so they are not so power-oriented, not so demanding and autocratic.

It is doubtful that anyone is born with a genetic predisposition to abuse a child physically. It is a learned behavior just as self-esteem is learned. It is possible to teach people a more respectful attitude toward children. They can learn to overcome their use of power, fear, and intimidation. When parents become frustrated and begin to use power, they should seek immediate help from someone who can teach them to give up the power. Too many parent programs still teach that subtle forms of violence used sparingly and "at the right time" are not risky, but research disagrees with this view. Every child has a different saturation point for sustaining violence.

Too many parents are saying, "I never thought he would turn out that way." Even worse, far too many do not care how their youngsters turn out. This neglect and other forms of child abuse have become a national disaster, just now coming to the surface.

Day care centers, unheard of forty years ago, essentially have within them the same attitudes of child rearing as do our schools. Minimum requirements for licensing are found in most states, and this should again tell us how we have a rather casual approach in developing our young people. There is no reason to believe that the environment for growth and development in these centers is any better than in our public schools. Can we believe that a teacher in a child care center might say to a parent of an unruly child, "If this was my child, I would turn him over my knee?" Expert day care will be needed in the twenty-first century or we risk continued poor development of youngsters nearing school age.

We seem to pass on the might-is-right attitude from generation to generation as easily as we pass on our traditional holidays. Child abuse is based on the top-down attitude that fear motivates. Fear does not motivate employees, at least in the long run, and it does not properly motivate our young people. It motivates them to find a way to balance the power being used on them . . . and they usually find a way. They are better at balancing the power than adults are at ridding themselves of it. The impression young people get, however, is that power works, and they undoubtedly use it in their relationships. Once again the old-fashioned, power-oriented method of development is passed on for others to use.

The fact is, we are either promoters of nonviolence or we are not. There just is not any in between on this issue. Many Americans see nothing wrong with slapping a child's hand when the child reaches for something he should not have. It is our custom either to remove the object or control the child by using physical abuse. It is better to remove the object or divert the child's attention. Parents know slapping gets quick results, and that is why they use it.

Most people would not correlate the same power-oriented attitude that promotes child abuse with the attitudes that are slowly weakening our corporations, our schools, and other institutions. The use of power, fear, intimidation, and humiliation are the bully-like traits that are taught to those people who abuse children. Even law enforcement officers sometimes promote physical abuse by the way they subdue suspects. A California court held that the officers who beat Rodney King did the right thing. It took the federal court system to overturn the decision and send the officers to prison. Similar tactics have been seen on television in large cities where officers have been overly forceful in controlling the suspect. Such actions intensify the use of power.

Physical child abuse can, in its worst form, create mental disorders that help form disturbed personalities. These personality difficulties are often not diagnosed quickly, and later on it takes a great deal of therapy to correct the disorders. In addition to the physical abuse, it is a tragedy that our spirit-killing words create disorganized personalities in young people. There is a wide range of personality disorders created by our autocratic methods of development, and some of these people are trying to function in our society. Many are contributing to the poor development of other people, and others are functioning on the edge of disaster in their lives.

Many states now have laws that mandate that teachers in schools and day care centers must report child abuse. This is a start, but parents and students (not teachers) are in the homes where abuse happens. If they suspect abuse, they should make reports to legal authorities.

Child abuse is the lowest form of mismanaging a person. It is caused by our culturally transmitted attitude that positional power carries with it an infinite right to intimidate, to get results regardless of the means. Many say the future of America is in the hands of our youth. We can significantly improve their development by making abrupt changes in the way we think about motivating and managing them and helping them grow.

Divorce—Spousal Abuse

Motivation and management within a family is at a low ebb when divorce is taking place. Divorce is still another clue that the traditional methods of establishing relationships in our culture are not based on the sound principles of what makes people find meaning in life. The use of power is ever present in those exchanges that bring about divorce. Our known spirit-killing words, put-downs, and poor confronting techniques help cause divorce. Judgments and analysis of a mate's behavior lead to diminished spirits in a marriage. Marriages lacking a reasonable understanding of good interpersonal communications and what true motivation is will be strained, often to the point of no return.

Since many people in marriages lack an understanding about true motivation, the abuse of power, and other spirit killers, tension builds between people just as it does between employers and employees, and teachers and students. Once the tension manifests itself, spousal abuse is often commonplace. It is now a national problem costing the United States plenty in terms of court time, absenteeism from work and, in severe cases, medical bills.

If a country is dependent on the stability of the family unit, the divorce rates in the United States should tell us we are headed for serious difficulty in the future. We can blame these discouraging rates on whatever we choose, but disagreements about money, sex, child rearing, and lifestyle cannot nearly cover the number of divorces caused by an inability to encourage, to trust, and not to use power. High-profile, autocratic spouses do not get any better results than high-profile teachers or managers when it comes to motivating people and establishing relationships.

Encouragement is the single most important aspect of any relationship.

Encouragement cannot be provided by using our typical forms of motivation. Marriage is an agreement to seek meaning in life together. The meaning breaks down when our autocratic, high-profile controls creep in because we continue to use pet phrases that chip away at someone's self-esteem or the control they have over the meaning in their lives.

The ability to be a little critical, give some negative feedback, and not strain a relationship is an art not well known by most people. Understanding that we cannot build up a relationship by starting to belittle weaknesses in another person is an understanding lacking in our society. Any relationship is in trouble when one person, perhaps unwittingly, takes it upon himself to make the other person become him. It is usually not practical to "mold" a personality to one we really think we would like instead of accepting some things we see as flaws.

Giving someone the space to grow and meeting someone's needs of gratification and recognition can help provide the love, empathy, and encouragement that constitute a good marriage. To control growth instead of letting it flow is, of course, a major cause of management failure in our country. There is little difference in why some marriages fail and why corporate giants or schools fail. They are mismanaged in terms of getting the best out of people.

Intimacy, fostered by encouragement, is placed on the back burner in our fast-paced, power-seeking society. Our special language can put intimacy back into marriages and significantly cut the divorce rate. Families that do not have to go through the agonizing divorce process can be on task and be more productive for America in the next century.

Few married couples seek divorce after thirty years of marriage. They have negotiated so many disagreements that there is nothing they cannot work out. They have, in their own way, created the special language and given up power that research tells us that successful companies, schools, and families have learned to do. Words of discouragement are seldom spoken. Weaknesses are no longer important when compared to the great strengths these couples can finally see in each other.

Divorce, spousal abuse, and all of the other clues our culture delivers to us should tell us we should stop doing those things that never work in human development and management of people. Shortly after taking office, in a televised speech, President Clinton said we should stop doing things that never work. He also said, "More Americans must contribute today so that all Americans can do better tomorrow."[47]

One might wonder in what way President Clinton was thinking that more Americans could contribute. Let us hope that the contribution would be in improving our human development and management skills because that is the best way "Americans can do better tomorrow." Keeping our autocratic businesses and schools alive by perpetuating a top-down style of managing and governing will keep America at risk in the twenty-first century. Our national debt is huge, but our biggest deficit is our autocratic style of motivating and managing people. We must change our thinking concerning this vital ingredient to help America become all it can be in the twenty-first century.

Appendix

Feeling Words

Pleasant Affective States

Love, Affection, Concern

admired	cooperative	helpful	nice
adorable	cordial	honest	obliging
affectionate	courteous	honorable	open
agreeable	dedicated	hospitable	optimistic
altruistic	devoted	humane	patient
amiable	easygoing	interested	peaceful
benevolent	empathetic	just	pleasant
benign	fair	kind	polite
bighearted	faithful	kindly	reasonable
brotherly	forgiving	kindhearted	receptive
caring	friendly	lenient	reliable
charitable	generous	lovable	respectful
Christian	genuine	loving	responsible
comforting	giving	mellow	sensitive
congenial	good	mild	sympathetic
conscientious	good-humored	moral	sweet
considerate	good-natured	neighborly	tender

From Gazda, G. M. et. al., *Human Relations Development: A Manual for Educators,* © Allyn & Bacon, 1973. Reprinted, adapted by permission.

Love, Affection, Concern *(continued)*

thoughtful	trustworthy	warm	wise
tolerant	understanding	warm-hearted	
truthful	unselfish	well-meaning	

Elation, Joy

amused	exalted	humorous	serene
at ease	excellent	inspired	splendid
blissful	excited	in high spirits	superb
brilliant	fantastic	jovial	terrific
calm	fine	joyful	thrilled
cheerful	fit	jubilant	tremendous
comical	gay	magnificent	triumphant
contented	glad	majestic	turned on
delighted	glorious	marvelous	vivacious
ecstatic	good	overjoyed	witty
elated	grand	pleased	wonderful
elevated	gratified	pleasant	
enchanted	great	proud	
enthusiastic	happy	satisfied	

Potency

able	durable	influential	spirited
adequate	dynamic	intense	stable
assured	effective	lionhearted	stouthearted
authoritative	energetic	manly	strong
bold	fearless	mighty	sure
brave	firm	powerful	tough
capable	forceful	robust	virile
competent	gallant	secure	well equipped
confident	hardy	self-confident	well put together
courageous	healthy	self-reliant	
daring	heroic	sharp	
determined	important	skillful	

Unpleasant Affective States

Depression

abandoned	despised	horrible	pathetic
alien	despondent	humiliated	pitiful
alienated	destroyed	hurt	rebuked
alone	discarded	in the dumps	regretful
annihilate	discouraged	jilted	rejected
awful	disfavored	kaput	reprimand
battered	dismal	left out	rotten
below par	done for	loathed	ruined
blue	downcast	lonely	rundown
burned	downhearted	lonesome	sad
cast off	downtrodden	lousy	stranded
cheapened	dreadful	low	tearful
crushed	estranged	miserable	terrible
debased	excluded	mishandled	unhappy
defeated	forlorn	mistreated	unloved
degraded	forsaken	moody	valueless
dejected	gloomy	mournful	washed up
demolished	glum	obsolete	whipped
depressed	grim	ostracized	worthless
desolate	hated	out of sorts	wrecked

Distress

afflicted	constrained	grief	perplexed
anguished	disgusted	helpless	puzzled
at the feet of	disliked	hindered	ridiculous
at the mercy of	displeased	impaired	sickened
awkward	dissatisfied	impatient	silly
baffled	distrustful	imprisoned	skeptical
bewildered	disturbed	lost	speechless
blameworthy	doubtful	nauseated	strained
clumsy	foolish	offended	suspicious
confused	futile	pained	swamped

Distress *(continued)*

the plaything of	tough	unlucky	unsatisfied
the puppet of	ungainly	unpopular	unsure
tormented			

Fear, Anxiety

afraid	fearful	jittery	shy
agitated	fidgety	jumpy	strained
alarmed	frightened	nervous	tense
anxious	hesitant	on edge	terrified
apprehensive	horrified	overwhelmed	terror-stricken
bashful	ill at ease	panicky	timid
desperate	insecure	restless	uncomfortable
dread	intimidated	scared	uneasy
embarrassed	jealous	shaky	

Belittling, Criticism, Scorn

abused	diminished	maligned	scoffed at
belittled	discredited	minimized	scorned
branded	disdained	mocked	shamed
carped at	disgraced	neglected	slammed
caviled at	disparaged	not taken seriously	slandered
censured	humiliated	overlooked	slighted
criticized	ignored	poked fun at	thought nothing
defamed	jeered	pooh-poohed	of
deprecated	laughed at	put-down	underestimated
depreciated	libeled	ridiculed	underrated
derided	made light of	roasted	

Impotency, Inadequacy

anemic	debilitated	exhausted	harmless
broken	defective	exposed	helpless
broken down	deficient	feeble	impotent
chickenhearted	demoralized	flimsy	inadequate
cowardly	disabled	fragile	incapable
crippled	effeminate	frail	incompetent

Impotency, Inadequacy (continued)

indefensible
ineffective
inefficient
inept
inferior
infirm
insecure
insufficient
lame

maimed
meek
nerveless
paralyzed
powerless
puny
shaken
shaky
sickly

small
strengthless
trivial
unable
unarmed
uncertain
unfit
unimportant
unqualified

unsound
unsubstantiated
useless
vulnerable
weak
weak-hearted

Anger, Hostility, Cruel

agitated
aggravated
aggressive
angry
annoyed
antagonistic
arrogant
austere
bad-tempered
belligerent
bigoted
biting
bloodthirsty
blunt
bullying
callous
cold-blooded
combative
contankerous
contrary
cool
corrosive

cranky
critical
cross
cruel
deadly
dictatorial
disagreeable
discontented
dogmatic
enraged
envious
fierce
furious
gruesome
hard
hardhearted
harsh
hateful
heartless
hellish
hideous
hostile

hypercritical
ill-tempered
impatient
inconsiderate
inhuman
insensitive
intolerable
intolerant
irritated
mad
malicious
mean
murderous
nasty
obstinate
opposed
oppressive
outraged
perturbed
poisonous
prejudiced
pushy

rebellious
reckless
resentful
revengeful
rough
rude
ruthless
sadistic
savage
severe
spiteful
stern
stormy
unfeeling
unfriendly
unmerciful
unruly
vicious
vindictive
violent
wrathful

References

Chapter 1: The Unseen Enemy

1. A manager should be well enough developed as a human being to handle what a situation requires . . ." and "One of the things . . . ," Pascale, R., *The Art of Japanese Management*, as cited in Walek, G., Author tells why Japanese managers get things done, *The Daily Herald (Arlington Heights, IL)*, September 8, 1981.
2. For a country built on individual freedoms we sure are full of loopholes," Russell, W. F., *Second Wind*, Random House, New York, 1979, 201.
3. "In the United States there is a fundamental mismatch between traditional American love of personal liberty . . ." and "Furthermore, traditional American management has adopted an insulting top-down approach . . . ," Naisbitt, J., *Megatrends*, Warner Books, New York, 1982, 181.
4. Ewing, D., *Harvard Business Review.*
5. "The reason behind the absence of focus on product or people in so many American companies, it would seem, is the simple . . . ," Peters, T. J. and Waterman, R. H., Jr., *In Search of Excellence*, Harper & Row, New York, 1982, 40.
6. Reich, R., *Think About It*, The Chicago Tribune.
7. "Karl Marx foresaw this distrust . . . ," Ouchi, W. G., *Theory Z*, Addison-Wesley, Reading, MA, 1981, 5.
8. "Man is a stubborn seeker of meaning," Gardner, J. W., *Morale*, W. W. Norton, New York, 1978, 15.

Chapter 2: The Spirit Killers

9. "A true people orientation can't exist unless there is a special language to go with it" and "The larger context of high performance, we believe, is intrinsic motivation," Peters, T. J. and Waterman, R. H., Jr., *In Search of Excellence*, Harper & Row, New York, 1982, 260, 72.
10. "Ordinary men . . . ," Egan, G., *The Skilled Helper*, Brooks/Cole Publishing, Monterey, CA, 1975, 17.
11. "A manager should be well developed as a human being to handle what a situation requires, not what the culture has taught him to be," Pascale, R., *The Art of Japanese*

Management, as cited in Walek, G., Author tells why Japanese managers get things done, The Daily Herald (Arlington Heights, IL), September 8, 1981.

12. "Millions of dollars . . . ," "So great is the demand . . . ," "It is not my purpose here . . . ," "The basic problem is . . . ," "Human personalities have a common characteristic . . . ," and "External motivation, whether reward or punishment . . ."; Cook, W., as cited in Dible, D. M., *Build a Better You—Starting Now!* Showcase Publishing, 1979, Fairfield, CA, 3, 13.

13. "Winners don't have a good attitude because they win; they win because they have a good attitude," Tunney, J., *Here's to the Winners,* audiocassette.

14. "The actual exercise of power . . ." and "Perhaps it is inevitable that coercive power generates the very forces that eventually will combat it . . . ," Gordon, T., *L.E.T.— Leader Effectiveness Training,* Wyden Books, 1977, 156, 165. Reprinted with permission.

15. "Dear Miss Carson . . . ," Goldstein W. and Devita, J. C., *Successful School Communication,* Parker Publishing, West Nyack, NY, 1977, 127.

16. "Frank is the kind of manager who . . . ," Morgan, J., "They Said It," *Sports Illustrated.*

17. "'With a person' rather than 'beyond a person,'" Carkhuff, R. R. and Berenson, B. G., *Beyond Counseling and Therapy,* by Holt, Reinhart & Winston, New York, 1967, 136.

18. "We live in a world in which we are all more able to discourage than encourage," Losoncy, L., *Turning People On: How To Be an Encouraging Person,* Prentice-Hall, Englewood Cliffs, NJ, 1977, x. Reprinted with permission.

19. "One wonders why . . . ," and Losoncy and Dinkmeyer compare discouragers and encouragers, Dinkmeyer, D. and Losoncy, L., *The Encouragement Book,* Prentice-Hall, Englewood Cliffs, NJ, 1980, 6–8.

Chapter 3: Top-Down Management: How It Fails Business

20. "Perhaps it is inevitable that coercive power generates the very forces . . . ," "Now that much of the mystery . . . ," and "It is one of the purposes of this book . . . ," Gordon, T., *L.E.T.—Leader Effectiveness Training,* Wyden Books, 1977, 165, 1–2. Reprinted with permission.

21. "Traditional American management has adopted an insulting top-down approach . . . ," Naisbitt, J., *Megatrends,* Warner Books, New York, 1982, 181.

22. "Giants begin to falter . . . ," Greenwald, J., "Are America's Corporate Giants a Dying Breed?" *Time,* December 28, 1992, 28.

23. "Somehow, over the years, we've been led to believe that . . . ," "We've got to get past a lot of this nonsense . . . ," and "Saddling someone else with the job of . . . ," Pritchett, P., *New Work Habits for a Radically Changing World,* Pritchett & Associates, 38, Dallas, TX, 1994.

24. "Today, world competition poses an organizational challenge . . . ," "A developing society . . . ," "There is no quick fix in sight . . . ," and "Mechanistic, programmatic solutions . . ."; Pascale, R. and Athos, A., *The Art of Japanese Management,* Warner Books, New York, 1981, 33, 31, 333.

25. "There is growing agreement ... " "If there has been any lingering doubt ... ," "In generations past ... ," and "There are now specialists who have unique power ... "; Ewing, D. W., *Do It My Way or You're Fired,* John Wiley & Sons, Inc., New York, 1983, 11, 2, 10.

26. "Until we believe that the expert ... ," "The language used in talking about people was different ... ," and "Don't ever lock this door again ... ," Peters, T. J. and Waterman, R. H., Jr., *In Search of Excellence,* Harper & Row, New York, 1982, 249, 16, 245.

27. "I want to work in a positive environment ... ," "We must learn how to talk with co-workers ... ," "It's really the responsibility of top management to ... ," and "Few people know how to give negative feedback ... "; Tarkenton, F., "Productivity and job satisfaction," April 1980. (An article by Fran Tarkenton, Chairman of the Fran Tarkenton Small Business Network.)

28. Reich, R., *Think About It,* The Chicago Tribune.

29. "The rules and assumptions about reduction ... " and "Life in the workplace for all Americans ... ," Downs, A., *Corporate Executions,* American Management Association (AMACOM), New York, 1995, 191, 199.

30. "C.E.O. philosophy ... ," Tsukamoto, K., One company's amazing road to labor peace, *Chicago Sun-Times,* November 29, 1981 (In an interview from *PHP Magazine*). Permission granted by "© PHP INSTITUTE, INC."

31. *N. Jones v. State of Illinois Educational Labor Relations and Illinois Federation of Teachers,* AFT, AFL-CIO.

Chapter 4: Top-Down Management in Education

32. "Teachers prepared kids ... ," Russell, B., *Second Wind,* Random House, 1979, New York, 3.

33. "Conventional classroom controls are not working ... ," "In short, conventional classroom controls are high profile," "All right, may I have your attention please?" "Look at me," "They are the norm," and "In nearly every United States elementary or secondary school ... ," Rinne, C. H., "Low-Profile Classroom Controls," *Phi Delta Kappan,* September 1982, 52.

34. "Perhaps it is inevitable that coercive power. ... ," Gordon, T., *L.E.T.—Leader Effectiveness Training,* Wyden Books, 1977, 165. Reprinted with permission.

35. "We ask kindergarten children" and "What happens along the way to people to make ... ," Losoncy, L., *Turning People On: How To Be an Encouraging Person,* Prentice-Hall, Englewood Cliffs, NJ, 1977, 50.

36. "There is a widespread lack of motivation ... ," "It is basically an authoritarian, and suppressive approach ... ," "Obedience is deceptive ... ," "Greater use of police departments to restore law and order ... ," and "Our future ... "; Etzioni, A., Students need self-discipline, The Chicago Tribune.

37. "Research has shown ... " and "Empathic teachers do not evaluate ... ," Long, L., *Listening/Responding—Human Relations Training for Teachers,* Brooks/Cole Publishing, Monterey, CA, 1978, vii, 3.

38. Reagan, R., in a speech to The National Assoc. of Secondary School Principals.

39. "It would be more meaningful..." and list of suggestions for creating a democratic atmosphere, Dreikurs, R., Grunwald, B. B., and Pepper, F. C., *Maintaining Sanity in the Classroom,* Harper & Row, New York, 1982, 91, 76.

Chapter 5: Top-Down Management: Effects on the Family

40. "Every child . . . ," Clark, F. A.

41. "Their experiences as children," "Observing the rules of order," "Our autocratic tradition . . . ," "A child who sees himself . . . ," and "We see discipline as growth . . ."; Dinkmeyer, D. and McKay, G., *Raising a Responsible Child,* Simon & Schuster, New York, 1973, 18, 107, 99, 11.

42. "To the extent that you have to rely on the authority . . . ," Ewing, D. W., *Do It My Way or You're Fired,* John Wiley & Sons, Inc., New York, 1983, 250.

43. If parents could learn only one thing . . . ," Gordon, T., P.E.T.—*Parent Effectiveness Training,* Peter H. Wyden, New York, 1975, 158.

44. "The money would come if we believed in our heart . . . ," Blackman, A. and Nayeri, F., "Where Children Come First," *Time,* November 9, 1992, 58.

45. "It is inevitable that coercive power . . . ," Gordon, T., *L.E.T.—Leader Effectiveness Training, Wyden Books,* 1977, 165. Reprinted with permission of Wyden Books.

46. "Self-esteem is confidence and satisfaction . . . ," "When I was growing up . . . ," "This myth about productivity . . . ," "The findings indicate quite clearly . . . ," and "First recognize someone's weaknesses . . ."; Blum, G., *Impact 84* (Institute for Family Research and Education, Syracuse University), no. 7, 1984.

47. Clinton, W. J.

Index